Galatians

Westminster Bible Companion

Series Editors

Patrick D. Miller
David L. Bartlett

Galatians

FREDERICK W. WEIDMANN

WESTMINSTER
JOHN KNOX PRESS
LOUISVILLE · KENTUCKY

First edition
Published by Westminster John Knox Press
Louisville, Kentucky

12 13 14 15 16 17 18 19 20 21—10 9 8 7 6 5 4 3 2 1

Book design by Publishers' WorkGroup
Cover design by Drew Stevens

Library of Congress Cataloging-in-Publication Data

Weidmann, Frederick W.
 Galatians / Frederick W. Weidmann. — 1st ed.
  p. cm. — (Westminster Bible companion)
 Includes bibliographical references (p.   ).
 ISBN 978-0-664-25814-6 (alk. paper)
 1. Bible. N.T. Galatians—Commentaries.   I. Title.
 BS2685.53.W45   2012
 227'.4077—dc23

                                   2011040041

Most Westminster John Knox Press books are available at special quantity discounts when purchased in bulk by corporations, organizations, and special-interest groups. For more information, please e-mail SpecialSales@wjkbooks.com.

Contents

Series Foreword

This series of study guides to the Bible is offered to the church and more specifically to the laity. In daily devotions, in church school classes, and in listening to the preached word, individual Christians turn to the Bible for a sustaining word, a challenging word, and a sense of direction. The word that Scripture brings may be highly personal as one deals with the demands and surprises, the joys and sorrows, of daily life. It also may have broader dimensions as people wrestle with moral and theological issues that involve us all. In every congregation and denomination, controversies arise that send ministry and laity alike back to the Word of God to find direction for dealing with difficult matters that confront us.

A significant number of lay women and men in the church also find themselves called to the service of teaching. Most of the time they will be teaching the Bible. In many churches, the primary sustained attention to the Bible and the discovery of its riches for our lives have come from the ongoing teaching of the Bible by persons who have not engaged in formal theological education. They have been willing, and often eager, to study the Bible in order to help others drink from its living water.

This volume is part of a series of books, the Westminster Bible Companion, intended to help the laity of the church read the Bible more clearly and intelligently. Whether such reading is for personal direction or for the teaching of others, the reader cannot avoid the difficulties of trying to understand these words from long ago. The Scriptures are clear and clearly available to everyone as they call us to faith in the God who is revealed in Jesus Christ and as they offer to every human being the word of salvation. No companion volumes are necessary in order to hear such words truly. Yet every reader of Scripture who pauses to ponder and think further about any text has questions that are not immediately answerable simply by reading the text of Scripture. Such questions may be about historical and geographical details or about words that are obscure or so loaded with meaning that one cannot tell at a glance what is at stake. They may be about the fundamental meaning of a passage or about what connection a particular text might have to our contemporary world. Or a teacher preparing for a church school class may simply want to know: what should I say about this biblical passage when I have to teach it next Sunday? It is our hope that these volumes, written by teachers and pastors with long experience studying and teaching the Bible in the church, will help members of the church who want and need to study the Bible with their questions.

The New Revised Standard Version of the Bible is the basis for the interpretive comments that each author provides. The NRSV text is presented at the beginning of the discussion so that the reader may have at hand in a single volume both the Scripture passage and the exposition of its meaning. In some instances, where inclusion of the entire passage is not necessary for understanding either the text or the interpreter's discussion, the presentation of the NRSV text may be abbreviated. Usually, the whole of the biblical text is given. We hope this series will serve the community of faith, opening the Word of God to all the people, so that they may be sustained and guided by it.

From almost the beginning of our work on the Westminster Bible Companion, Stephanie Egnotovich of Westminster John Knox Press was our editor, encourager, and friend. Her death was a great loss to us and to this project, and with gratitude we dedicate these volumes to her memory.

Introduction

"It's not about you." That's a mantra for some educators who lead workshops and otherwise work with pastors or seminarians who are studying to be pastors. And it's good advice because, indeed, it is not about the given church leader and the identifiable (and, for that matter, unidentifiable) gifts and particulars that he or she brings to a given position. It's about God, mission, the gospel, and the church. The advice, "it's not about you," at its best, serves to protect and support both the individual leader and the local and broader church.

But—there's always a "but"—it *is* about the church leader at some level, isn't it? All that she or he brings to a particular place and position will vary from what any other individual brings and is informed by upbringing, education, vocations and avocations before the call to ministry, current commitments both within and outside of the church, and a plethora of social markers. And further, it is a commonplace within many churches that teachers or preachers will comment from time to time—if not often—on their own tastes, foibles, and life experiences in order to illustrate or prove a point. Many reading this book will recognize themselves, or a beloved colleague or church leader, in that last sentence.

All of which leaves us at an important place in approaching this extraordinary letter from a person at once so familiar and yet, in significant ways, so distant, mysterious, challenging, and even confusing. To return to our mantra above, how does Paul negotiate the distinction between the "it" of his calling, mission, and gospel and the "you" of his own self and identity? And, to the degree he fuses, or confuses, himself with the broader mission, why does he do so? How are we, the readers/hearers/recipients, *now*, to react? How did they (Paul's first hearers), *then*, react to Paul and his message? Such questions are particularly appropriate and, along with many others, will guide our reading of Paul's Letter to the Galatians.

1

GALATIANS AMONG THE EPISTLES OF PAUL

Galatians is a part of the collection of Paul's letters within the New Testament. We know from Paul himself (2 Cor. 2:3–4) and from other ancient sources that Paul wrote letters beyond those which are preserved for us in the New Testament. To complicate matters further, as indicated in the *Colossians, Ephesians, First and Second Timothy, and Titus* volume within this series, those particular letters are considered by many modern scholars not to have been composed by Paul himself but by those within later communities wishing to speak with the authority of Paul. So, simply defining or describing the collection of Paul's letters is not as easy a task as it may at first seem.

We know for sure, at least by scholarly consensus, that Romans, 1 and 2 Corinthians, Galatians, 1 Thessalonians, Philippians, and Philemon are the "undisputed" (a term used by many scholars) letters of Paul. Galatians, of course, is among these.

This volume considers Galatians, Paul's angriest letter, and one in which he gives a sustained autobiographical sketch. Galatians was written to a Christian community that Paul had been active in founding. That said, "Christian" is a designation not found in Galatians, and which, as far as we know, Paul did not use. Galatians was written "from the field" after Paul had left and moved on to another site in his ongoing missionary work and church development.

IDENTITY

Above, I raised a question about Paul's "own self and identity." Paul speaks to that question very directly and repeatedly in Galatians. Several things mark who Paul was *and continued to be*. Why do I add emphasis to the second half of that sentence?

Many speak of Paul's "conversion," and on the face of it the designation makes sense. Within Paul's letters, particularly in the autobiographical sections of Galatians and Philippians, it is evident that Paul separates his life into two distinct portions: before his encounter with Christ and after. Once God had "called" him to a new life and mission, he dropped everything and "went away" (Gal. 1:15–17) from his former life, both literally and figuratively. Further, he even writes that he counts "all gains" from his pre-encounter life to be "loss" or "rubbish" (Phil. 3:6–8). Many who have had "conversion" experiences themselves, or know individuals who have, will recognize such behavior and descriptions. That said, we who read and associate ourselves with Paul and his message need to be careful both about the language we use and what it means.

Does conversion mean leaving your religion? Paul didn't do that, at least according to descriptions in the book of Acts (roughly half of which is devoted to descriptions of Paul and his ministry) and in Paul's letters. Paul remains committed to, and associates with, Jews and Judaism throughout, as we see in Romans 9–11 and in Galatians, despite, or perhaps because of, Galatians's very strong language. That Paul's movement is a mission *within* Judaism is a position that has been in the ascendancy for decades and has gained consensus status among scholars to the point where it now makes "common sense." Both Christian and Jewish scholars—whose work independently and, with continuing benefit and insight, together—agree. It is true historically and socially. A simple glance at the book of Acts will indicate Paul's continued interaction with synagogue communities. So too is it true theologically (as is confirmed within the letters themselves). Paul could not conceive of himself or his ministry outside of Judaism and Jewish Scripture, patterns of thought, and behavior.

But what about Paul's "conversion"? It remains a good and descriptive word for Paul and Paul's ministry provided we have some clarity about what it does and doesn't mean. The work of Alan Segal is particularly influential is this area of Pauline studies (*Paul the Convert*; and, later, "Response: Some Aspects of Conversion and Identity Formation"). According to Segal, "Paul is a convert in the basic sociological sense of that term—a person who changes religious communities. That does not necessarily have to apply to changing from one religion to another. . . . Paul continues to be a Jew and he continues to believe that his new faith is part of Judaism" ("Response," 185). In this book, I will refer both to Paul's "conversion" and, using a word closer to his own description, to his "call" (Gal. 1:15).

Beyond his own identity, Paul is much more concerned with the corporate identity of individuals and communities who/which are formed and defined "in Christ": ". . . for in Christ Jesus you are all children of God through faith. As many of you as were baptized into Christ have clothed yourselves with Christ. There is no longer Jew or Greek, there is no longer slave or free, there is no longer male and female; for all of you are one in Christ Jesus" (Gal. 3:26–28). The working out of what this means for Paul's mission, for the individuals and communities addressed, and for the broader mission and spread of "the gospel" sets the agenda, in one way or another, for Paul's letters. Community identity, from the foundational and all-encompassing definition of Galatians 3:28, is "in Christ." What is true for Paul is true, so he hopes and asserts, for the community: ". . . it is no longer I who live, but it is Christ who lives in me. And the life I now live in the flesh I live by faith in the Son of God, who loved me and gave himself for me" (Gal. 2:20).

MISSION

Closely tied to identity is mission. Why was Paul converted or "called" (Gal. 1:15) but to "proclaim" that which God revealed to him (Gal. 1:16)? The loaded (because of its contemporary application to those who had known, and ministered with, Jesus) term that Paul uses for himself, "apostle," at its root means "one who is sent (on a mission)," as is evident in the NRSV translation of Galatians 1:1: "Paul an apostle—sent neither by human commission nor from human authorities, but through Jesus Christ and God the Father. . . ." There is, in fact, no verb "sent" in Galatians 1:1; that sense is understood simply from the use of the noun, "apostle."

Paul is nothing if not an apostle, an ambassador, a person on a mission, and everything works for and toward that end. The movement through the autobiographical/mission sketch in Galatians 1–2 indicates as much in its pointed transition words, each marking a new chapter or episode: "Then after three years" (Gal. 1:18), "Then after fourteen years" (Gal. 2:1), and ". . . when Cephas came" (Gal. 2:11).

END TIMES

Though hardly steeped in language and imagery or even, at first glance, concerns of the end times, Galatians does indeed start of off with a very pointed term regarding the end times: "revelation." And, Paul repeats it as if to suggest that it should not be missed: (1) ". . . for I did not receive [the gospel] from a human source, nor was I taught it, but I received it through a revelation of Jesus Christ" (Gal. 1:12); (2) "[God] was pleased to reveal his Son to me, so that I might proclaim him among the Gentiles" (Gal. 2:15–16). Here, in no uncertain terms, the reader of Paul encounters the purpose and context of Paul's mission: to proclaim Jesus Christ among the Gentiles. That is what God has *revealed* to him *through a revelation* and such a mission is consistent with what Paul knows of the end times given his study of, and familiarity with, Scripture and tradition. Paul is living and working and informed by "the end times."

THE TIME IS NOW

I am aware, as I write these words, that "the end times" has a very particular connotation in our popular entertainment and news media. One thinks of particular and peculiar images informed by particular and peculiar readings of the book of Revelation, including individuals being suddenly raptured into heaven. Further, one thinks of a callous disregard toward the world that some who, in our times, are informed by the end times assume. Suffice it to say that, as I hope is clear from the discussion above, such is not Paul's, or his tradition's, notion of the end times. As discussed in greater detail in the *Philippians, First and Second Thessalonians, and Philemon* volume in this series, when Paul writes in Philippians 3:20 that "our citizenship is in heaven, and it is from there that we are expecting a Savior, the Lord Jesus Christ," he is not checking out or urging others to check out from their relationships with and for each other and for the world. Quite the opposite, he is urging the very direct and ongoing engagement of individuals within the community, and of the community with the world.

I am also aware of the very influential "existentialist" impulse in biblical scholarship and in American religion, which is often (and, for the most part, correctly) associated with the New Testament scholar Rudolf Bultmann, that focuses on the individual/individual's engagement of Scripture and the urgent call and pull that that engagement can have on the individual. There is much to commend that impulse and much that is positive in biblical scholarship and in American religious expression that has come from it. It can also lead to a kind of theological blindness.

When I title this short section, "The Time is Now," I mean neither to suggest that the end of the world is coming in a "the sky is falling" sort of way, nor do I mean to suggest—at least not solely—that a deep and certain moment of truth awaits the individual who would encounter, or be encountered, by God; though I should hasten to add that given the choice of those two alternatives, I would tend toward the latter, and do so with enthusiasm. What I do mean to suggest, and underline, is that for Paul the time has come and is now for the (reconstituted?) people of God to respond to the gospel. As sure as is the case stated above with regard to Galatians 3:26–28—that the "working out of what this means for Paul's mission, for the individuals and communities addressed, and for the broader mission and spread of 'the gospel' sets the agenda, in one way or another, for Paul's letters"—so is the case with this notion that for Paul the time has come and is now for the people of God to respond to the gospel. Indeed, the two are the same.

And so Paul challenges his congregations, other congregations, his tradition and those who engage—and are engaged by—it, his opponents (who, like him, would be included among those who engage—and are engaged by—his tradition), potential converts, and all who would listen that the time has come and is now to respond to the gospel message *as the people of God*. And so he writes to communities about life in community in and for the world. The time is now for God's people to constitute themselves/itself as God's people and respond, and live, and preach, and teach, and act accordingly. No easy task! For Paul it was worthy of never ending prayerful care and effort. May our own engagement of Galatians be a continuing part of that effort.

PAUL'S LETTER TO THE GALATIANS

Galatians is in some sense both the least and most representative of the letters of Paul, and—this is the interesting part—one could point to some of the same characteristics to prove either case. Of course, that says more about how Paul has been read and understood than it does about Paul himself or about the Letter to the Galatians per se. It also says something about the complexity, depth, and passion of this letter and the subjects it treats.

Topics addressed in the letter include "the Law," "Faith," "Grace," "the Jews," and "Abraham," to name a few. Each of these is considered by many interpreters to be quite characteristic of Paul and essential to his message. That may be so. Indeed, each plays a key role in Paul's longest and perhaps best known and most highly revered letter, the letter to the Romans.

But it is also important to note that these topics are seldom, if ever, addressed in any of Paul's other letters besides Galatians and Romans. And further, the way that the vast majority of readers—scholars, preachers, laypersons—have traditionally understood and, to a significant degree, continue to understand Paul's treatment of some of these topics, and the terms and concepts that define them, may not jibe with Paul's presumptions or those of his early readers. In short, the Protestant tradition has tended to understand and promote the core of Paul's message as a call for faith and a depiction of grace which stands over, against, and in reaction to, the presumed "works-righteousness" inherent in Judaism. Yet, as we will see in the readings and discussions below, the notion that "Judaism" is, as a whole, something over and against which Paul stands is an orientation unthinkable to Paul and incongruous to his message.

And so, as we read and engage Galatians, we tread on hallowed and disputed ground. What can be said for certain is that we are privileged to be able to engage and draw inspiration for our own individual and community lives of faith from this passionate letter written to real people in real time for the purpose of addressing and resolving real and central concerns of mission and life together.

That said, we cannot know for certain from where, and to whom, the letter was written. The former matter may seem understandable, as neither the title nor the body of the letter name a place of origin. But what of the latter concern? Clearly the letter indicates that its addressees are "the Galatians." What more identification do we need?

As a former New Yorker, I can reply that labels—even ones that may seem precise—often contain ambiguity. If a religious leader were to write a letter to "New York" or to "the New Yorkers," could we be certain whom, or what geographical region, that letter was meant to address? Perhaps it would address those in the whole state; perhaps only those in New York City; perhaps, within the city, the addressees would be limited to Manhattan (excluding the other or "outer" boroughs that make up New York City proper). Once we had settled on a choice from among those possibilities, we would then ask the further question of what particular community or communities, within the broader designation, the letter addressed. This little exercise begins to approximate some of the difficulties in sorting out Paul's addressees.

Galatia had at least two distinct and overlapping designations at the time of Paul's writing. First, it referenced the territories historically occupied by the "Galatian" peoples. These were ethnic Celts who had made their way east from Europe into central Asia Minor (west-central Turkey on today's map) during the third century BCE. They developed several cities in the Anatolian interior, including a capital at Ancyra (modern day Ankara, the capital of Turkey). During the early establishment of the Roman Empire, Galatia was formally annexed as a province of the empire. At the same time it was also expanded by Rome to include regions to the south that were formerly and historically separate and distinct from Galatia, including Pisidia and parts of Lycaonia and Phrygia (names familiar to those who have read or heard about Paul's travels as outlined in the book of Acts). The first of many questions to be addressed, then, is whether Paul was writing with the more limited region of historical Galatia in mind or with that of the broader Roman provincial designation.

A stickier and more expansive question is hinted at in the parenthetical phrase above regarding the book of Acts. Acts, most of the second half of which is dedicated to Paul and his mission, contains many details about Paul and his travels. Many of these details are, on the face of it, consistent with what we know from Paul's own letters. Others are variously more challenging to align with Paul's own testimony (so far as we have it in the letters). On the matter of identifying "the Galatians," the material from Acts may fill in some of the blanks that Paul's letters present while also complicating other matters. What do I mean?

A number of places named within the account of Paul's first and second missionary journeys in Acts 13–14 and 16:1–5 fall within provincial Galatia: Pisidian Antioch, Iconium, Lystra, and Derbe. While these places are not named in Galatians (or any of the other letters of Paul) they do represent potential stops for someone, like Paul, who was working his or her way through the province. It would be reasonable, offhand, that one or another (or a set) of these cities could account for the communities to which the letter is addressed. But there is more that indicates another, stronger possibility.

In the body of the letter, Paul refers directly to his listeners, indeed one might argue that he cries out to them, with the label, "You . . . Galatians" (3:1). Such a label, and in particular such use of that label, suggests that Paul's listeners would have indeed considered themselves, and been considered by others, to be historically and ethnically "Galatians." That is more likely the case if Paul is writing to the northern, historically Galatian, part of the province. On a related note, description within the body of the letter indicates that the communities addressed are Gentile (see esp. 4:8–9); that is, they are not Jewish or, via Jewish members, partly Jewish. Though the existence of a strictly Gentile community or set of communities is by no means impossible in a region that is known to have included Jewish populations (such as the southern areas of provincial Galatia at Paul's time), the apparent lack of Jews within the community(ies) Paul addresses lends further plausibility to the conclusion that Paul's addressees are, indeed, northern, historically ethnic Galatians. On balance, it is likely that the letter is written to Gentile Christian communities within Ancyra and/or neighboring cities.

A related question about the location is the degree to which Acts describes both the broad and particular background and context for Paul's writing. Should one willy-nilly look to harmonize the information from the letters with the narratives, descriptions, and reports of Acts? Alternatively, should one look to Acts—which, after all, was collected and written by someone other than Paul, perhaps at an interval of time (and place) quite removed from Paul—with a critical, or even suspicious, eye? On many levels, the easy and obvious answer is to favor primary evidence (Paul's own testimony from his letters) over secondary evidence (accounts written about Paul in the book of Acts). This study will favor the testimony of Paul's letters while looking cautiously to Acts to help fill in gaps that Galatians and the other letters leave for us. That said, this commentary will also consider the agenda Paul may have in presenting his case as he does.

There are many gaps and no easy resolution to the matter of how Galatians jibes with the narratives of Paul's missionary journeys, the apostolic council described in Acts 15, and other debates with the Jerusalem-based leaders reported in Acts. This constellation of concerns rises to the fore in a consideration of Galatians 1–2, as Paul relates something of his complicated interaction with the "the pillars" in Jerusalem. Whatever the possible resolutions may be, it is clear that Paul is reacting to what he perceives as a significant threat to his mission *from within the fold of those who, like him, are dedicated to spreading the gospel*. Whether this perceived threat is connected to or otherwise informed by the famous apostolic council of Acts 15 or another (related?) meeting such as that described in Acts 18:22 is taken up later in the commentary.

When, and from where, Galatians was written are questions that have no easy answers. However, there are fairly sure boundaries within which to look. It is very likely that the letter comes from the middle of Paul's known letter-writing career, preceding both Romans, written in the late 50s, and the Corinthian correspondences (closer to the mid-50s). First Corinthians 16:1 suggests that Paul may have composed a second letter to the Galatians, which is now lost. In 1 Corinthians, Paul mentions that he gave instructions to the churches of Galatia about "the collection" for the churches in Jerusalem, but there is no mention of the collection in the Letter to the Galatians that we have. With relative certainty we can date Galatians broadly to the early to mid 50s, which allows, on the one hand, sufficient time for Paul's travels through the region and the subsequent agitation of other missionaries to gain—or, at the very least, threaten to gain—ascendancy among the Galatians; and on the other hand, it predates the whole matter of Paul's efforts on behalf of the collection for the churches in Jerusalem discussed in 1 Corinthians 16:1 (and elsewhere in the Corinthian correspondences and Romans). More specifically, it allows for Paul's extended stay in Corinth (the close of which can be ascertained via external evidence to the proconsulship of Gallio, 51–52 CE). At the *very* earliest, Galatians might have been written during that Corinthian residence. More likely is a date toward the earlier end of Paul's extended stay at Ephesus, where he would later be imprisoned. Since there is no indication in Galatians that Paul is imprisoned (as there is in Philippians and Philemon), this letter presumably precedes those letters and his imprisonment.

Among the items that support my earlier statement that Galatians is Paul's "angriest letter" is its lack of a thanksgiving section. This is notable on the face of things (since Paul's letters generally do include a thanksgiving), and the omission is certainly consistent with the tone of the body of the letter in which Paul is reacting to developments within the community that concern him greatly. In Galatians, Paul is not just angry, he is, as one of my seminary professors put it, "hopping mad." I don't think it is overstating the case to say Paul was fighting for the very life and integrity of his "gospel."

Consistent with such a fight, Galatians has with growing consistency (under the important influence of Betz's Commentary) been read by scholars as an "apologetic" letter: that is, one that follows to a significant degree the general form of a presentation within a court proceeding. Perhaps Galatians is best approached as an eclectic letter that borrows from a number of epistolary and other rhetorical genres, and is influenced by "apologetic" patterns of presentation and argumentation. In the classical sense, "apology" is a defense of oneself, and by extension, one's positions and actions. That accounts broadly for Paul's agenda herein. Further, and just as centrally, Paul means to define, describe, and display his understanding of the gospel. He means to persuade his addressees to adopt that understanding and act, as a community, accordingly. Like a freight train (not a "runaway," but one that is being engineered with purpose and determination), this letter leaves the station fast and furious and with one purpose: to deliver its content effectively and efficiently.

1. Salutation and Address
Galatians 1:1–5

1:1 **Paul an apostle—sent neither by human commission nor from human authorities, but through Jesus Christ and God the Father, who raised him from the dead—**[2] **and all the members of God's family who are with me,**
   To the churches of Galatia:
   [3] **Grace to you and peace from God our Father and the Lord Jesus Christ,** [4] **who gave himself for our sins to set us free from the present evil age, according to the will of our God and Father,** [5] **to whom be the glory forever and ever. Amen.**

PAUL, THE GALATIANS, AND GOD: TAKE ONE

Paul has a lot to accomplish in the opening lines of this letter, perhaps not least being able to harness his anger and frustration and to focus his words, descriptions, and arguments on the matters at hand. These include (1) (re)establishing his credentials and integrity; (2) illustrating the import and integrity of that which he preaches, that is, his "gospel"; and (3) persuading the Galatians to (re)embrace him and his gospel. From the start, Paul is equal to the task and shows little or no interest in entertaining lesser concerns or diverging from the task in any way.

Typical of Paul's—and most ancient—letters, this one begins with an epistolary introduction that includes the identification of the sender(s) and the addressee(s). So far, so good. As is true of many of Paul's letters, this one has multiple authors or senders; what is somewhat unusual in this case is that Paul's coauthors remain nameless (cf. 1 Cor. 1:1; 2 Cor. 1:1; Phil. 1:1; 1 Thess. 1:1; 2 Thess. 1:1; Phlm. 1). By referring to them as "members of God's family who are with me"—literally, as per the NRSV alternative reading, "all the brothers," or better, since the Greek word for "brothers," in the plural, serves the purpose of the universal to refer to a collective of siblings of both genders, "all the sisters and brothers" or "all the siblings"—Paul accomplishes at least one, and perhaps two, rhetorical goals: (1) he lays the foundation for the familial language, and the sense of familial relationship with God and within the community that he will be promoting within the body of the letter (especially, but not limited to, Gal. 3:26, 29; 4:1–7); (2) he leaves it open to suggestion, and to one's imagination, what the number and strength of his group of coauthors, colleagues, associates, and/or coworkers is (two? several?).

Of course, the names of the coauthors are not the most obvious of what is missing. As discussed in the introduction, the opening of Galatians is notable and unique (though see 2 Cor.) within the Pauline corpus for its lack of a thanksgiving. Is it that Paul just didn't like his addressees or have anything much to be thankful about with regard to them? Even were one to entertain either or both of those possibilities, a reading of the letter would soon dismiss them. Paul was, as a matter of fact, quite moved by the Galatians and the reception and treatment he received among them (4:12–15). But therein may lie the rub! No sooner does his reminiscence touch on the deep affection he felt then he counters: "have I turned into an enemy to you?" (4:16). The feelings are strong, and so are the stakes ("the gospel" itself, 1:6–7). That combination may well explain this pointed, thanksgiving-less, salutation.

Further, Paul displays what might be taken as a sense of urgency and intensity about the purpose—and strategy—of the letter. As indicated in the introduction, Galatians unfolds much as an "apology." And so it begins in what appears to be a defensive or apologetic mode as Paul indicates (1) what he is—"an apostle"; probably countering charges to the contrary; (2) what he is not—one commissioned by human authority or institutions; probably suggesting that his rivals do fit into that category *and, further, that they are not divinely commissioned like him* (at least, not in Paul's opinion); and (3) why and how he rightfully considers himself to be divinely commissioned, "through Jesus Christ. . . ."

The phrase ". . . through Jesus Christ and God the Father, who raised him from the dead" is important and should not be passed over too quickly for its apparent familiarity. First, there is the stated presence of both "Jesus" and "Christ." As is indicated so clearly in Philippians 2, in both the introduction to (2:1–5) and recitation of the Christ Hymn (2:6–11), for Paul the one necessarily presumes the other—"Jesus," quite literally, embodies Christ, and "Christ" as divine being, power, and inspiration presumes "Jesus." Further, all the above happens within the sphere of "God the Father." That is, Paul does not refer to, or presume, isolated activity by Jesus Christ, and that is certainly the case with the resurrection. Jesus, or Jesus Christ, does not raise himself from the dead (as is often presumed or stated within many mainline and evangelical Christian settings and as is affirmed—within many denominations and local church bodies— in the regularly recited words of both the Apostles' and Nicene Creeds: ". . . on the third day he [Jesus Christ] rose again from the dead"). Rather, as stated in Paul's first (1 Thessalonians) and last (Romans) letters, and several times in between, the resurrection occurs not through Jesus Christ's own action but rather by direct action of "God the Father" (Rom. 4:24–5, 8:11, 10:9; 1 Cor. 6:14, 15:15; 2 Cor. 4:14; 1 Thess. 1:10).

Notable too is the particular language that Paul uses here and elsewhere. As he will share just a few verses further on (see esp. 1:14–15; also Phil. 3:5–6), Paul not only associates himself with Judaism and Jewish piety and scholarship broadly, but also with a particular tradition or set of traditions therein, namely Pharisaism. Pharisaism is directly associated with the rabbinic movement within Judaism that developed the scholarly base (Mishnah and Talmud) and liturgical expressions that we associate with Judaism today. The Amidah, or Eighteen Benedictions, is the daily prayer in Judaism, with roots in the same first-century Pharisaism with which Paul identifies himself. In the second benediction of the Amidah, God is referred to as "the one who raises the dead." Has Paul borrowed, recast, or refocused onto Jesus Christ a devotional line, which he prayed and perhaps continued to pray every day? Though scholars endlessly debate the date when the Amidah was codified—and certainly Gamaliel II, who thrived in the decades *following* Paul's death, played a key role in that codification—there is little doubt that something closely resembling the text of the Amidah as we know it was regularly recited within the Pharisaic movement during Paul's lifetime.

Interestingly, Paul first introduces this parental phrase with no modifying word at all; indeed, even the "the" before "Father" is not stated in the Greek text. However, "Father" comes up two more times in the address (vv. 3 and 4), each time with the modifier "our." It is worth noting that in the Greek text, the modifier is literally closer and more directly related to "Father" than is captured in the English translation of verse 4. But then, how might one more accurately translate that phrase? As it stands, the NRSV translation presumes a distributive sense of the "our," which, in the Greek, follows directly on the word, "Father": so, in a sense, "our God and our Father." Alternatively, one could take the whole phrase following "God" to be further and directly modifying "God": so, ". . . God [who is] also our Father," along with being Jesus' father. What makes that translation attractive in rendering Paul's language is its consistent focus on the "our" as a modifier of "Father," and on the kinship rhetoric (already visible in v. 2) with which Paul builds and models understanding of Christian community with and under God. The phrase itself, "our Father," is reminiscent not only of Jesus' own devotional address in the Lord's Prayer (Matt. 6:9), but of several passages within Paul's letters (Rom. 1:7; 1 Cor. 1:3; 2 Cor. 1:2; Phil. 1:2, 4:20; 1 Thess. 1:3, 3:11, 13; 2 Thess. 2:16; Phlm. 3).

PAUL, THE GALATIANS, AND GOD: TAKE TWO

Now that Paul has (re)established who he is and (re)oriented his listeners to the kinship and community they can and should feel with Paul, each other, and God and begun to recall and reframe for his listeners who and what Jesus Christ and God are for them, he moves forward with a positive statement of greeting or salutation: "Grace to you and peace." That core greeting is then modified by a complex line, in terms of both content and grammar, which reinforces much of the content of the first two verses.

The core greeting here is quite standard for Paul (Rom. 1:7; 1 Cor. 1:3; 2 Cor. 1:2; Phil. 1:2; 1 Thess. 1:1; 2 Thess. 1:2; Phlm. 3)—which is not to say that it lacks meaning or substance. Quite the opposite, Paul's first word of choice, "grace," arguably looms large for Paul and his theology, especially in the particular letters of Romans and Galatians (see comments on 1:6, 2:21, and 5:4, below). Its repeated use by Paul in his letters' addresses reflects a simple, but creative, modification of the standard word for "greeting" regularly found at the beginning of a standard Greek letter. Paul's use of "grace" is, of course, pointed to his addressees and to his and their relationship to God and God's action on their, and the world's, behalf. And further, while the first word gives a nod to Greek salutary convention, the second, "peace," favors a broadly Semitic or distinctly Jewish idiom, recalling the "*shalom*" greeting (see, example, Dan. 4:1) standard in epistolary and other addresses. That Paul enjoyed and found meaningful this balance of "grace" and "peace" is indicated by the way he employs various modifications of the greeting in Galatians and other letters, often by balancing phrases within just a few verses of each other that use one element or the other (e.g., Gal. 6:16, 18; Phil. 4:9, 23; 1 Thess. 5:23, 28; 2 Thess. 3:16, 18).

The content of verses 3–5 regarding Christ's action is dense. In verse 1, "Jesus Christ" was named first and then "God the Father," with the balance of the sentence given to describing action by the latter. Here the sentence unfolds in precisely the opposite manner, with the balance of the sentence describing action by *and* directing glory toward Jesus Christ.

Another difference is the addition of a phrase embedded within the description of Jesus Christ's action that refers back to "God our Father."

Regarding Jesus Christ, the sentence includes such descriptions and concepts as "giving himself" for our "sins" to "free" us from the "present evil age." As already noted in the introduction, that last phrase in particular indicates apocalyptic understanding and framing on Paul's part. In some way, his message is about the end times and contains a sense of urgency meant to move his listeners to a new understanding or grasp of reality.

Recall that our whole discussion about Jesus Christ and God, and God's action through Jesus Christ, began via a quick outline of Paul's self-presentation and definition as "an apostle." As indicated in the introduction, the word "sent," as found in the English of the NRSV and many translations, does not even appear in the Greek text; it is embedded in the noun "apostle," which means, literally, "sent one." And Paul—as opposed to others, one wonders (see esp. comments on 2:1–10 below)—is not sent or commissioned by any human institution or authority but directly through Jesus Christ and God the Father.

The description is reminiscent of a standard description of the true Cynic, or moral philosopher, as found, for example, in the writings of Epictetus, a younger contemporary of Paul's. The true teacher is "sent (that is, "apostled") by God." And why is the teacher sent? ". . . in order to show [humans] that in questions of good and evil they have gone astray, and are seeking the true nature of good and evil where it is not, but where they think" (Epictetus, *Discourses*, 3.22.23). Paul's message is otherworldly; it is about God and God's action. Paul means to orient, or reorient, his readers to the truth—God's truth.

As one sent by God, Paul speaks for God. He is in the role of announcing and offering grace and peace from God (v. 3). He further renounces the current age as "evil," marked by "our" sins (v. 4). In so doing, he not only parallels, to some degree, Epictetus's model of the true moral philosopher but also draws on deep and particular traditions within Judaism.

Perhaps the handiest description of the current, "evil," age found within biblical literature (as broadly defined to include the apocryphal books of the Old Testament) is in 2 Esdras, also known as *4 Ezra*, beginning with 7:12. Therein the descriptions of "this world" include such terms as "sorrowful," "toilsome," "evil," and "full of dangers." And as one reads on in that text one finds that the those who live in "this world" were characteristically "not obedient, . . . spoke against [God], . . . devised for themselves vain thoughts, and proposed to themselves wicked frauds; they even declared that the Most High does not exist" (2 Esd. 7:22–23). These characteristic behaviors are "sins," a word that occurs no less than ten times in the chapter, and perhaps most programmatically and ominously in verse 68: "For all who have been born are entangled in iniquities, and are full of sins and burdened with transgressions." Paul uses fairly typical language of conversion ("formerly, . . . you did not know God") to describe the situation of the Galatians prior to his missionary activity among them (4:8). One can well imagine Paul employing something akin to the language of 2 Esdras in his missionary teaching; though, perhaps, modifying it somewhat for a Gentile audience. Now, on the far side of that originating missionary activity and following a period in which "some" other teachers (1:7)—drawing on some of the same deep Jewish traditions that Paul did—have been active among the Galatians, Paul is able to use brief descriptions as a kind of shorthand. His readers are aware of the "evil" age and the sorts of activities and nonactivities that "our sins" denotes.

That said, Paul uses "sins" in the plural only this one time in Galatians and only two other times in the extant letters (1 Cor. 15:3, 17; cf. Rom. 7:5, "sinful passions"). Further, both this occurrence and 1 Corinthians 15:3 fall within what appear to be traditional confessional statements (likely predating Paul, and learned by him in Christian communities established prior to his missionary activity, such as that in Antioch), while the third, 1 Corinthians 15:17, is clearly a comment on the earlier confessional statement in 15:3. When not quoting such confessional material, Paul consistently uses "sin" in the singular (Gal. 3:22; 4:3, 7, 8, 9, 24; 5:1). In what ways might recognition of that pattern affect popular notions of "sin" or "sins" among our churches? Within Paul's letters, and in this one particularly, the more characteristically Pauline usage arguably underscores one of Paul's theological presumptions: namely, that sin, as a dominating force in "the present evil age," has a hold on people; hence, the "prisoner" and "slave" imagery from Galatians 3:22; 4:3, 7, 8, 9, and 24.

Notably, and consistent with verse 1 above (God the Father as actor), the closest parallels to the phrase, "who gave himself for our sins," are either passive (Rom. 4:25)—suggesting that another, in other words, God, is the actor—or directly indicate that God is the actor (Rom. 8:32). Again, consistent with our discussion about the phrase in verse 1, either of the options employed in Romans seem the more natural way for Paul to express the matter. That the one other example using this same phraseology comes again in this letter, "gave himself for me" (Gal. 2:20), suggests even more strongly that Paul is here using traditional confessional language (perhaps also employed in Galatia by the other teachers). Though the contexts and precise subject are different (here regarding the earthly death of Jesus; in Phil. 2:7, regarding the so-called kenosis, or empty-ing, of the divine Christ into human existence), the pattern of active verb (gave; emptied) followed by reflexive pronoun (himself; himself) is consis-tent with the Christ Hymn, which is also a traditional confessional com-position predating Paul.

Many have seen in this early confession regarding Christ's death close parallels or similarities to contemporary Jewish texts. Were such the case, it would not be surprising, because early Christian communities and mis-sions, Paul's included, were developing within Judaism and drawing on Jewish scriptures and other traditions to understand and communicate God's action through Jesus. Among the texts most often cited by schol-ars is 2 Maccabees 7:32, 37–38, which recounts the gruesome tale of the serial executions and martyrdoms of seven Jewish brothers under the Syr-ian king Antiochus, who ruled in the mid-second century BCE. In the dramatic telling of the death of the final son, within the trialogue among himself, his mother, and the evil king, the son states, ". . . we are suffering because of our own sins." He then goes on to suggest something akin to a redemptive effect that his, and his brothers', deaths might have on the cause of saving the Jewish nation: "I, like my brothers, give up body and life for the laws of our ancestors, appealing to God to show mercy soon to our nation . . . and through me and my brothers to bring to an end the wrath of the Almighty that has justly fallen on our whole nation." Is Christ's action, according to the confession herein, akin to that which these brothers enact and for which the final brother appeals? Arguably, yes. At the very least there are basic similarities in terms of cause ("our . . . sins") and response ("gave himself"; "give up . . . life").

What of effect? According to 2 Maccabees, it is "to bring to an end the wrath of the Almighty." According to Paul herein, the effect is "to set us free." The term here translated, "free," though unique in Paul's letters, is highly nuanced and perhaps familiar on a couple of levels. Within the Jewish biblical tradition, this is a standard term for "freeing" or "deliver-ing" someone from someone or something (as in Exod. 18:4, which recalls the period of Pharaoh's hold over the Israelites). Within common Greek parlance, the term was used to refer to gaining the status of a "freedman": that is, becoming a former slave, now freed. Both senses are consistent with Paul's discussions in the body of the letter, in which he will consider the closely related themes of slavery and freedom often (see esp. 4:1–7, 4:31–5:1, 5:13).

We have paid a lot of attention to the particular phraseology of these confessional statements regarding Jesus Christ in verse 4 and noted their dissimilarity to Paul's more characteristic statements. As if to bring this confessional statement into the Pauline sphere, Paul adds the phrase "according to the will of our God and Father," or, as indicated above, "according to the will of God [who is] also our Father." To repeat my comment above regarding the resurrection as recalled in verse 1, all happens within the sphere of "God the Father." That is, Paul does not refer to or presume isolated activity by Jesus Christ. For Paul, all that Jesus Christ is and does is via "the will of our God. . . ." This phrase itself is unique in Paul. Usually, when Paul invokes God's "will," it is regarding human behavior or activity (see, example, Rom. 12:2 and 1 Thess. 5:18, the latter of which also includes reference to "Jesus Christ"), including Paul's own apostolic calling and missionary movements (Rom. 15:32, 1 Cor. 1:1, 2 Cor. 1:1).

2. The Occasion for Writing
Galatians 1:6–9

1:6 **I am astonished that you are so quickly deserting the one who called you in the grace of Christ and are turning to a different gospel—** [7] **not that there is another gospel, but there are some who are confusing you and want to pervert the gospel of Christ.** [8] **But even if we or an angel from heaven should proclaim to you a gospel contrary to what we proclaimed to you, let that one be accursed!** [9] **As we have said before, so now I repeat, if anyone proclaims to you a gospel contrary to what you received, let that one be accursed!**

NO THANK YOU

Both in the introduction to this letter and near the top of the discussion about the salutation and address, we noted that Galatians, uniquely among Paul's letters (though see 2 Cor. 1:11, with its somewhat inverted "thanks," from "many" on behalf of Paul), has no thanksgiving section. Paul gets right to the point! Though a real level of anger and emotion may well be at play, Paul proceeds with purpose and skill, setting up a framework of characters and (counter)charges, and a language of genuineness versus perversion, which will carry through the body of the letter. And front and center, as it was in the salutation, is Grace.

The book of Acts famously records Paul saying that he is from "no mean city" (21:39). That is indeed the case. Besides boasting an important Mediterranean port and inland routes to the Anatolian heartland, a diverse population and centers of learning, and a recent past that includes the fabled story of Cleopatra and Antony meeting on the gilded barge, Tarsus also served as a provincial seat under the Roman republic and, for a time in the mid-first century BCE, hosted as governor to none other than the famous rhetorician Cicero. In his own discussion of how to structure an apology, or defense, Cicero advises the discrediting of one's opponents. He also makes a point of indicating the importance of addressing that which one's opponent deems of central importance and of showing some "perplexity and astonishment" (Cicero, *De inventione rhetorica* 1.17.25). Paul seems to proceed along these lines.

Clearly this section serves to discredit those teachers who, also Jewish (like Paul) and also Christian (like Paul), had come to be with the Galatians to forward their preaching and teaching. There is no direct consideration here of their particular teaching or approach or identification of them by name or title. They are simply "some." And not only do they "pervert" or change that which Paul teaches, they even "want" or "will" to do so. What is also notable, within Paul's description, is that the word "want" hearkens back to the same word (translated "will," v. 4) that he has just used regarding God. Clearly, for Paul, these teachers are not doing the work of God; what they "want" is not what God "wants"; they are not spreading the "gospel" of the action of Jesus Christ as willed, or wanted, by God.

Their modus operandi is to "confuse" their listeners, which they, at least from Paul's standpoint, have apparently effectively done. The term is a loaded one, which suggests notions of "unsettle" or "disturb," as we shall see. The same word is used in the extended narrative about the Jerusalem Council in Acts 15 to describe "certain persons," presumably from Jerusalem, who "have said things to disturb you [Gentiles] and have unsettled your minds" (Acts 15:24). That the same word is used of Paul's opponents in Galatians 1:7 and of those "certain persons" in Acts 15 is a literary connection that is unfortunately lost through the differing translations in the NRSV. The parallel is even closer when we recognize that "certain persons" translates as the same word, "some," that Paul also uses here.

So, does the Acts passage shed any light on these rival teachers? Yes. How much? At the very least, the Acts passage helps us construct a framework within which to situate these teachers and their rivalry with Paul. There is the common theme and goal of proceeding with mission work to and among Gentiles (non-Jews). But, how are Gentiles to be welcomed into the church, which still is situated within the fold of Judaism both in practice and association? Like the teachers referenced in Acts 15:24, Paul's rivals in Galatians are likely associated with the Jerusalem church *in some way* and clearly disagree with Paul's approach. They are his opponents; the Galatian church is their battleground; what is at stake is "the gospel"!

If we were to take the points gleaned from Cicero, above, as a kind of recipe or checklist, we might pause for a moment on the matter of "perplexity and astonishment." Clearly Paul indicates as much, in the very first statement of this section, "I am astonished." But who or what is he astonished at? The rival teachers? No, the Galatians themselves. That is a simple and important point and sets up much of the tension within the letter. Paul is not merely defending himself against opponents—rival teachers—in some rhetorically constructed court of law, and his addressees are not merely outsiders, or even a judge or jury, to the case. The matter is about Paul's "gospel" *and* about the Galatians, and the two are not easily separated; indeed, Paul would "perish the thought" that they be separated. And so, as much as Paul is defending himself and his "gospel" against the rivals' teachings, he is also looking to persuade his addressees (back) into the fold of his "gospel." Either objective—defending himself and his teaching against the rivals or winning back the Galatians—is a challenge. Paul chooses both.

So, Paul directly attacks, or at least lobs a charge (desertion) against his listeners: "I am astonished that you are so quickly deserting . . ." Though the English, "deserting," evokes for me, first, a military context (someone who goes AWOL has "deserted" his or her unit), the Greek word Paul chooses to use favors a context more related to association with a school or ethical approach. So, for example, in literature from this period when someone leaves one philosophical school for another, this term is used. Further, in early Christian literature, it was used more broadly to indicate something akin to conversion, a turning from evil to good. Here, it refers to a deconversion, if you will. These Galatians, who had been converted by Paul and joined his mission enterprise on behalf of the "gospel," are now (at least in his mind) setting that aside for something else. Interestingly, once in place ("you are so quickly deserting"), this charge against the Galatians is somewhat softened and refocused onto the rival teachers who, as we have already seen, are in the business of "confusing."

PAUL'S "GOSPEL"

Paul is again, like Epictetus's ideal teacher, central as "the one who called you. . . ." He is God's spokesperson, sent by God to spread this message. Paul is perhaps not so subtly reminding the Galatians that he is the one who founded their community. *He*, not that one or those others, is their teacher and his is the gospel message that they were to follow. What is the core of that message? Interestingly, here we find again the word, "grace."

Already in the introduction we have seen how "grace"—along with several other terms and concepts, such as "the law," "faith, "the Jews," and "Abraham"—is important, arguably even central, to Galatians and

Romans. And, of course, it has already shown up in the salutation, as it does in each of Paul's letters.

This phrase, "grace of Christ," is not found anywhere else in Paul's letters or in the New Testament as a whole. It appears as a kind of standalone and not, like some of the unique phrases in verse 4, as part of a confessional statement. What is more, the phrase "of Christ" does not appear in the earliest extant manuscript witness to this verse, which has many scholars wondering whether Paul wrote simply, "grace." If so, it would be consistent with other passages (like Gal. 5:4), which have an unmodified "grace." If "grace of Christ" is Paul's original wording, it presumably refers broadly to God's action through Jesus Christ as discussed above or, perhaps more pointedly, to that state of being in/within Christ (Gal. 1:22, 2:17, 3:29; see similarly 2:4, "in Christ Jesus").

The Greek phraseology that Paul employs here can either mean *in* the grace of Christ, as our English translation renders it, or *by* the grace of Christ. That is, the preposition can have either a locative (where) or an instrumental (how; by what means) sense. Perhaps the built-in ambiguity of the Greek phrase fits Paul's agenda well: it is by or through grace that he called the Galatians, *and* it is from within grace that he called/calls them into the same state. If one presumes that it must mean one or the other, then given the repeated revisiting of the locative sense throughout the letter, as shown in the list of citations above, I would favor that sense, consistent with the NRSV translation, as the one Paul has in mind here.

But what of "grace" itself. What is it and how, if at all, is it central to Paul's message? At 2:21 and 5:4, its only other uses in Galatians besides this verse and the address, it stands in contrast, or opposition, to "justification . . . through the law" (2:21; "justified by the law," 5:4). Can we assume such a contrast here? Perhaps. Paul is clearly countering a move away from his "gospel" and toward the rivals' teachings. He does so by anchoring his message—that to which the Galatians have been "called"—in "grace." So far, so good.

What precisely is Paul's understanding of grace in opposition to? The standard and easy answer, for those (consciously or not) familiar with the overwhelming trend in Protestant theology, is to contrast grace with "the law" and see these as reflecting two distinct theological approaches to God and answers to the human condition. The law, and in particular the "works-righteousness" that it engenders, so the argument goes, is modeled in Judaism; it is the wrong way to go. Grace, freely given by God (so that all we must do is accept) is modeled in Christianity; it is the right way to go. The rival teachers are Jewish, and they are wrong.

There are several problems on several levels with that position, perhaps most simply is its mistaken identifying of the teachers vis-à-vis Paul. As we have seen, these are not Jewish teachers versus a Christian Paul. Rather, and consistent with Acts 15 and other narratives about rival groups within Christianity, these are rival *Christian* teachers. The debate here is not about Jewish Law versus Christian Gospel. As noted already, it is about understanding and applying the Christian gospel to a still fairly new reality, which Paul and others are pushing: the presence and assimilation of Gentile converts or adherents within Christian communities.

Next is the misunderstanding of Judaism that this standard approach engenders. Simply put, Judaism is posited to be, in a sense, grace-less, whatever that might mean. The prophet Jeremiah, of course, knows no such thing, as he speaks the word of the Lord: "The people who survived the sword found grace in the wilderness; when Israel sought for rest, the LORD appeared to him" (Jer. 31:2). The sectarians at Qumran are often considered to be extremists when it comes to following (at least some aspects of) the law, and they were certainly not followers of Paul or adherents of Christianity. Yet, within their writings are found "Thanksgiving Hymns" that contrast what might fairly be called "works-righteousness" with reliance on God's grace: "For Thou knowest the inclination of Thy servant, that I have not relied [upon the works of my hands] to raise up [my heart]. . . . [Thy servant has] no righteous deeds to deliver him from the [pit of no] forgiveness. But I lean on . . . Thy grace" (1 QH VII.11). Neither the debate between Paul and his opponents reflected already within the first verses of Galatians (grace versus another approach) nor its terms pit Christianity against Judaism.

Third, there is the misunderstanding of Paul's position that the standard reading has engendered. Neither Paul nor Paul's understanding of "grace" stands willy-nilly against the law. Paul does indeed stand strong against many things related to the law or given interpretations of the law: for example, the rivals' desire to apply (at least part of) the law in Paul's opinion, to the Galatians. But his often nuanced arguments and the broad and specific points they are developed to make on behalf of his "gospel" are easily lost if we assume the standard Protestant reading. For now, let's take Paul at his word: this "grace," this gift, of God is something directly related to, and driven by, God's action through Jesus Christ.

Unlike "grace," Paul's use of "gospel" does, or at least might, suggest exclusivity. Now, whether Paul is comfortable with that is an important question. He might be crossing a line; one can almost feel it as he moves from phrase to phrase: "a different gospel," "not that there is another gospel," "a gospel contrary to what we proclaimed to you," and "a gospel contrary to what you received." Is there only one gospel for which Paul and others serve, *or* are there contrasting and competing gospels? It seems that Paul might be working out an answer to that question right before our eyes, leaning in the direction of (potentially) exclusive gospels in Galatians (see 2:7) while embracing the idea of one gospel movement (albeit not without difficulties) in Philippians (1:15–18).

That said, Paul is generally comfortable with designating his mission and message as "gospel," and uses the term consistently for that purpose throughout the letters (e.g., Rom. 1:16; 1 Cor. 4:15, 9:23; 2 Cor. 8:18; Phil. 1:5, 2:22, 4:3; 1 Thess. 2:4). In Galatians 2:2 he references specifically "the gospel that I proclaim among the Gentiles" (see again 2:7; cf. Rom. 11:25–28).

As many readers of this volume will know, the basic (non-Christian) meaning of the Greek term generally translated "gospel" is "good news." And news is, even if written down, generally delivered in the ancient world by messenger. What is lost in translation, but hinted at in the NRSV's alternate reading, "messenger" (footnote "b" in 1:8), is the connection between the word for "messenger," or "angel," and the word "gospel." This translation might capture it: "But even if we or a messenger from heaven should proclaim to you a message contrary to that which we proclaimed to you, let that one be accursed." Paul is waxing somewhat rhetorical. But that said, he is also coming down hard in favor of the enduring truth of the "good news" that he preached to the Galatians. Even if I and those with me change our own minds, don't listen. In something of a (momentary) spin on the opening words of the letter, Paul is—just to make the point—removing himself from the position of authority as one sent by God and putting in that place the gospel that he had preached.

Nor should we pass too quickly over Paul's cohort in crime within this rhetorical flourish. According to the NRSV translation (which, finally, is to be preferred for the very matter about to be discussed), it is "an angel from heaven." Reading from the distance that we do, we need to be careful not to gloss over this too quickly. As has already been observed, Paul is writing in what he understands to be the end times. He, like all associated and familiar with Jewish apocalyptic thought at the time, is familiar with angels and roles that they play in the end times. A handy, and telling, example can be seen in Revelation 14:6: "Then I saw another *angel* flying in midheaven, with an eternal *gospel* to proclaim to those who live on the earth—to every nation and tribe and language and people" (emphasis mine). The possibility that Paul posits is one genuinely available to him and available to other teachers and communities versed in Jewish apocalyptic traditions and, presumably, available to his hearers who have been trained by him. Indeed, the rivals may—we cannot be certain—have claimed for themselves some relationship with angels and/or a message received from heaven.

Finally, the related statement in Galatians 3:19, "[the law] was ordained by angels through a mediator," which may seem remarkable to us, was simply taken for granted by many in Paul's day. Why? Because the Bible said so. In Moses' retelling of the Sinai narrative in Deuteronomy 33:2, the Hebrew text appears to indicate that God was accompanied by various divine attendants, with a particular group or rank named as being "at God's right side," or "on [God's] right hand." In the Septuagint, a standard Greek translation of the Hebrew Bible that was widespread in Paul's day, this somewhat obscure group was simply identified as "angels." The rival teachers, whether claiming authority from a current or recent encounter with angels or with a new message from heaven, may have made reference to angels' presence at Moses' reception of the Law at Sinai. If so, that might account for Paul's reference here. Regardless, given the biblical and apocalyptic contexts it raises, this passing, though telling, reference to "an angel" moves Paul's readers in several directions at once: the end times (confirming other phraseology he has already used), the law (yet to be directly addressed), and God's various ways of communicating with God's people.

Like the angels, the curses might be written off as merely rhetorical flourish or even, perhaps, as superstition. They are neither, though Paul again may feel he is nearing, or crossing, a line. By including himself and his colleagues in this hypothetical scheme—"even if we or an angel . . ."— he somewhat softens the direct evoking of a curse. Nonetheless, it is a curse, and it is stated twice, in precisely the same language, lest we miss it or miss Paul's seriousness in using it. As for the language used, it has so infused our language that it doesn't even need the NRSV's translation— "accursed" translates the Greek, "anathema." Consistent with the reference to angels, Paul may well be drawing on the Greek language of the Septuagint (see, e.g., Deut. 7:26). Furthermore, simply in the stating of the curse with regard to the situation in Galatia, he is treating the Galatians as a sacred community with biblical roots and suggesting that they see themselves as such.

3. On the Defensive
Galatians 1:10–12

1:10 Am I now seeking human approval, or God's approval? Or am I trying to please people? If I were still pleasing people, I would not be a servant of Christ. [11] **For I want you to know, brothers and sisters, that the gospel that was proclaimed by me is not of human origin;** [12] **for I did not receive it from a human source, nor was I taught it, but I received it through a revelation of Jesus Christ.**

Paul's words in verses 10 and 11–12 are transitional in the clearest sense: they repeat and open up some of the key points and themes he has already established, and they move the reader into the body of the letter, in which Paul and Paul's gospel will be defended via discussion of his calling, training and background, and career *and* via discussion of the content of the gospel—what it is and what it includes and what it is not and does not include.

To set these verses apart from either the preceding or subsequent text, as they appear here, is arguably artificial. Clearly they belong with what precedes. Or, would it be more accurate to say, clearly they belong with what follows? Or, would it be best to separate them, 10 and 11–12, from each other (as in the NRSV and many translations)? No answer is fully satisfactory and that is, I imagine, just as Paul would have it; these are, as already noted, truly transitional verses. Isolating them allows us to focus on how Paul, at this key point in the letter, affirms and develops his presentation.

The first of these verses sets up a kind of mock court. Paul is on trial to determine whose approval he is seeking. There are two possibilities given. He is either trying to please God or people. The answer is, perhaps, obvious—God. End of story. Or is it?

The first of the two questions above uses a particular Greek word, which Paul will revisit later in the letter (5:8, "persuasion"). On the face of it, it is innocent enough: "persuade." The first question in verse 10 reads, literally: "For now am I persuading people or God?" What is wrong with "persuading people"?

First, as has already been noted, Paul has a twofold purpose in writing this letter: defending himself and his gospel against rival teachers and persuading the Galatians to (re)adopt his gospel (see, e.g., Gal. 3:1-2). So, insofar as the Galatians are people, is he not trying to persuade them? Perhaps. But he never uses that word with regard to himself or his mission. Why?

"Persuade" had come to take on a negative connotation in Greek moral philosophy or in teaching circles more generally, and could be lobbed as a criticism. "Persuading" is what those others—who were untrustworthy—did. It suggested activity that might, in our way of thinking and talking, be considered "slick" or "fast" or "blowing smoke." "All that glitters isn't gold," I was told as a kid. And those who tried "to persuade" seemed to put a lot of rhetorical gold (via their smooth talking or promises) on display. So, when Paul states later that "[s]uch persuasion does not come from the one who calls you" (5:8), he is affirming verse 6, that he is "the one who called you in the grace of Christ, and furthering the implied sense that it is not he, but they—the other teachers—who are not to be trusted.

There is a wonderful parallel to verse 10 in Paul's earliest extant letter. He writes in 1 Thessalonians 2:4, "but just as we have been approved by God to be entrusted with the message of the gospel, even so we speak, not to please mortals but to please God who tests our hearts." This provides significant insight into Paul, his teaching, and mission. First, the contents of Galatians 1:10 are clearly not simply a surface or constructed-on-the-fly reaction to the situation at Galatia or to charges that the rival teachers may well have lobbed at him. No, such argumentation was part of Paul's repertoire. Second, it betrays (in the positive sense of that word) Paul's foundation in Jewish religious piety. Of course Paul says that he is no faker, no charlatan. Who wouldn't? Charlatans most of all would claim not to be charlatans! But notice that Paul is fixed, securely, in his own religious stance and in deep religious tradition. His words in 1 Thessalonians recall Jeremiah 11:20: "But you, O LORD of hosts, who judge righteously, who try the heart and the mind. . . ." Paul is not a *re*actor, merely reacting to charges. He takes direct action—spreading the gospel—anchored in his own religious conviction. One could even imagine that something akin to 1 Thessalonians 2:4, or even Jeremiah 11:20 itself, was stated by Paul as part of his original teaching to the Galatians.

Paul closes out verse 10 by referring to himself as—and strongly suggesting that he is—"a slave," not servant, "of Christ." Here the alternative

NRSV reading, "slave," is to be favored over "servant." Why? For the simple reason that Paul was writing within a slave society; one whose economic and social structure presumed, and depended on, slavery. And he uses a word meaning, simply and straightforwardly, "slave." That "slave" was also a term used in Scripture (again, likely read and heard just that way—as "slave") furthers the argument for preferring the alternative reading. Is "slave" an uncomfortable word for us, given the history of slavery in the United States and elsewhere, and the (illegal, but nonetheless still occurring and even growing) trafficking of certain populations in the United States and around the world today? I hope so.

Was this label, "slave of Christ," like the discussion of pleasing God or pleasing people, part of Paul's repertoire? It is possible. Paul directly calls himself a "slave of Christ" (NRSV alternative reading) in Romans 1:1. Of course, unlike the matter regarding "pleasing God," we cannot be sure that Paul was already, at the time of writing Galatians, using that label for himself, since Romans is written after Galatians. What we do know for sure is that the label is consistent with, and helps to set up and develop, a central theme within the letter.

That said, Paul's own use of the slavery-freedom motif might seem less than consistent. He has, after all, just written about the action of Jesus Christ, which "sets us free" (v. 4). Why now invoke slavery in an apparently positive sense? A balance—or dissonance (?)—is struck in chapter 5, which begins with the statement, "For freedom Christ has set us free" and moves within several verses to "through love become slaves to one another" (5:13). Inconsistency? Maybe. Or perhaps Paul is summoning his listeners, their actions, and even their language to a higher calling.

Paul will directly address his own calling beginning in the very next verse (1:11) and proceeding through verse 12 and beyond. The "slave of Christ" self-reference transitions his readers toward that discussion as it recalls scriptural descriptions of the prophets. Perhaps foremost among these are Jeremiah 7:25 and Amos 3:7, which, in different ways, prefigure the discussion to follow: loud echoes of Jeremiah are felt in verse 15, while the Amos quote may well directly undergird verse 12.

Verse 11 serves as a kind of second beginning to the letter or, to be more precise, it arguably begins the body of the letter. Paul addresses his readers directly, using the same familial designation for them that he uses for his coauthors and close associates in verse 2. The alternative reading of the NRSV includes "brothers" in both places, indicating Paul's use of the same Greek word (see broader comments about translating this term in the discussion of v. 2, above).

The strong beginning to the verse, "I make known" or "I am making known" or, to push the Greek just a little bit, "I will make known," is masked a little by the NRSV translation. Further, the NRSV translation, with its use of "want" (recall that in the discussion of v. 7 we saw that "want" in v. 7 and "will" in v. 4 translate the same Greek word), suggests a connection with two earlier phrases in verses 4 and 7 that is simply not there in Paul's original wording. His statement is self-standing and self-referential: "I am now, and will throughout the letter, make known . . ." .

That which Paul does and will make known has already, more or less, been stated (in and around verses 1, 7, and 10, for example): what he preaches is not "from" humanity. The word "from" here is best understood as *in accordance with*, or *according to*, or *characteristic of*; the Greek here allows for, and even suggests, one or more of these. That is, again, what Paul preaches does not, nor is it meant to, "please" humans over God. More pointedly, it does not agree with, nor is it characteristic of, the human. There is something different about Paul's gospel! The wording is clipped, and surely it is meant to be: there is no word after "human" in Paul's Greek; it simply stands there alone: "human."

The gospel is particularly highlighted in this verse through the use of the same Greek root—*euangelion*—for both the noun, "gospel," and the verb, "proclaimed": literally, ". . . the gospel, the one gospelled by me. . . ." To say the least, Paul does not shy from that word, and, apropos of the discussion regarding "gospel" in verse 6, he claims it as his own.

The beginning of verse 12 directly picks up on the matter of the non-humanness of Paul's gospel expressed in verse 11. On the face of it, the first two phrases make sense: "I did not receive if from a human source, nor was I taught it." What may be missed by readers today is the technical language that Paul is employing here *and* the interesting and complicated relationship this language has to another of Paul's statements. To our ears, "receive" may seem a simple enough word. Particularly within the Pharisaic tradition in which Paul was trained, it would grow to have great significance, as is alluded to in Galatians 1:14. These are the opening words of the *Pirke Avot*, or *Fathers of Rabbi Nathan*, a foundational tract within rabbinic Judaism that came to be placed at the beginning of the Mishnah: "Moses *received* the law from Sinai, and he handed it down to Joshua, and Joshua to the elders [the Judges], and the elders to the prophets . . . " (*Pir. Avot.*, 1.1; emphasis mine), and so on. Paul's word for "receive" is equivalent to the words both for "received" and "handed on." That is, the word Paul uses itself suggests just such a chain of tradition as this foundational rabbinic text records.

So, what is the problem with tradition? We don't know (yet). We do know that, consistent with verse 11, Paul means to emphasize that his gospel is not consistent with "human/humanity." Perhaps one can now fill in, or fill out, that phrase a little bit: Paul's gospel is not consistent with human tradition or (a certain) human institutionalized observance such as is codified through a chain of tradition.

The complication around Paul's use of this term "receive" is exacerbated when we note that in 1 Corinthians 15:1 he begins a seemingly very different discussion using language that is almost word for word the same as the language he has just used in verse 11: "I make known to you, brothers and sisters, that the gospel which I preached [or literally, "gospelled"] to you, and which you received . . ." (1 Cor. 15:1; my translation). Notice the last phrase includes the same technical term that Paul uses in Galatians 1:12: "receive." Two verses later, in 1 Cor. 15:3, Paul expounds on that word: "For I handed on to you as of first importance *what I in turn had received*. . . ." (NRSV; emphasis mine). Does Paul in 1 Corinthians 15:1–3 contradict what he writes here in Galatians?

Of course, the two passages come from different times (1 Corinthians being later) and speak to different circumstances. Two quick points can be made regarding the 1 Corinthians passage. First, though the technical language—"had received"—strongly suggests as much, Paul nowhere in 1 Corinthians 15 states that he received the tradition that he hands on *from somebody/ies* who is/are *human*. Second, within the 1 Corinthians passage Paul does appear to affirm the story as he recalls it in Galatians: "Last of all, as to one untimely born, he appeared also to me" (1 Cor. 15:8 NRSV).

The language at the close of verse 12 is strong and pointed: "I received it through a revelation of Jesus Christ" (NRSV). And here, Paul may even be showing some playfulness with tradition. He "did not receive" his gospel in the normal, human way; he has "received it"—same technical term, typically denoting, as we have seen, a tradition passed on from person to person and generation to generation—"through a revelation" from God. Notice too that it places Paul in the position of Moses, who "received" the law at Sinai—according to the *Pirke Avot* passage quoted above; and on that score recall that in the discussion above we may have already heard some passing reference to that Moses event in Paul's inclusion of "an angel" in verse 8.

But we may be getting ahead of ourselves. Paul seems to have already set a context for understanding "revelation," which is different than that of Moses at Sinai, as has already been suggested through his use of "slave of Christ" in verse 10. Just as that phrase might call to mind, among the prophets, Amos 3:7, so now that particular passage rings loudly in the readers' ears: "Surely the Lord GOD does nothing, without revealing his secret to his servants the prophets" (NRSV). It will not surprise the reader of this study to know that the word behind "servants" in the ancient Greek version of the Old Testament, the Septuagint, already discussed above, is the same as that which Paul uses in the phrase, "slave of Christ." Like the biblical "slaves the prophets" (Jer. 7:25; Amos 3:7), so Paul as "slave of Christ" receives a "revelation" from God. And just like the charges of the good teacher, according to Epictetus, so too the charges of Amos "do not know how to do right" (Amos 3:10). Like the good teacher *and* like the prophet, Paul is called directly by God to right God's people.

We have already encountered several times the potential tension between action by Jesus Christ and action by God the Father. And, as we have seen, Paul consistently favors the latter. That is, for Paul, God is the actor (as in Gal. 1:1), or, at the very least, Christ's actions are "according to the will of our God" (Gal. 1:4). The question of the relationship of "revelation" to "Jesus Christ" raises an analogous question: is this a revelation that Jesus Christ enacted, or is it a revelation enacted by God the Father whose object is Jesus Christ or whose content is regarding Jesus Christ?

The Greek grammar, like the NRSV translation, is ambiguous on this matter and provides no easy answer. In this case, however, broader context seems to provide a ready answer. In verses 15–16 Paul recalls that "God . . . was pleased to reveal his Son to me." Presuming that verse 12 is consistent with verses 15–16 and consistent with Paul's broad understanding of divine action, then verse 12 is better translated, "through a revelation about Jesus Christ."

Finally, this language of revelation places us again in the realm of apocalyptic literature and understanding. As already indicated, we readers lose something if we do not take that seriously. We also lose something if we presume various popular understandings of apocalyptic, or the apocalypse, in our own world. This is Paul's first of four uses of "revelation/reveal" (1:12; 1:15–16; 2:2; 3:23), the first three of which are in rather quick succession within autobiographical narratives about the spread of Paul's mission. How is God's "revelation" world changing for Paul, for preaching, for those to and for whom it is preached, and for the world, or people, in general? How, by way of allusion to both Epictetus and Amos, does it reveal what is wrong and how to make it right?

4. Paul and the Prehistory of His Mission
Galatians 1:13–17

1:13 **You have heard, no doubt, of my earlier life in Judaism. I was violently persecuting the church of God and was trying to destroy it.** [14] **I advanced in Judaism beyond many among my people of the same age, for I was far more zealous for the traditions of my ancestors.** [15] **But when God, who had set me apart before I was born and called me through his grace, was pleased** [16] **to reveal his Son to me, so that I might proclaim him among the Gentiles, I did not confer with any human being,** [17] **nor did I go up to Jerusalem to those who were already apostles before me, but I went away at once into Arabia, and afterwards I returned to Damascus.**

Paul has a lot of ground to cover. One might have thought, given that Paul founded these churches and spent time with them, that it is ground he would have already covered. Perhaps so. But some time has, and some other teachers have, intervened. Paul variously needs to set the record straight or reframe some of his past history and stories to meet the needs of the present situation. He also needs and wants to develop matters that his introductory material has suggested and introduce new information for his readers' consideration.

"If Paul hadn't been born, we'd have had to make him up," you can almost hear a Hollywood producer or some such figure say. Simply on face value, let alone their context in this letter, these descriptions are colorful and capture the imagination. My own favorite image—for its excess—was at a particular holy site I visited while tracing Paul's life, in which Paul was being remembered as a persecutor. It had him dressed in full military regalia (but not so full that a few rippling muscles wouldn't show) commanding a brigade of soldiers: a kind of Arnold Schwarzenegger-like commander. On the one hand it seemed a very silly portrait; on the other it simply extrapolates, in a certain twentieth-century Western militaristic and cinematic direction, what Paul leaves to the imagination. Given various frames of reference and regardless of how one might fill out this portrait, its placement and usage within the letter seem to serve some particular purposes.

This is indeed prehistory. Paul speaks a limited number of times about his past in the letters we have (besides Gal. 1:13–2:14, see Phil. 3:3–8; cf. also 1 Cor. 15:8–10 and 2 Cor. 11:21–12:13, esp. 11:22, 12:1–4). His reasons for doing so vary. Here he is, at the very least, establishing the heavenly radicalness of his gospel. He never would have come to it on his own via his own training in the traditions that had shaped him. No. And a number of things prove that.

First, he was not open to or enticed by Christianity. Quite the opposite, he was "persecuting" it "in excess" (the Greek word here, which has come over into English as our word "hyperbole," may take on the meaning "violently" given its relationship to "persecuting.")

What form Paul's actions against Christian communities took is unclear. We can look to chapters 8 and 9 of Acts to fill out the portrait, but the relationship between the relevant passages in Acts 8 and 9 and Paul's own statements is strained. In Acts 8:1–3, Paul—therein still named Saul—appears at the center of a "severe persecution" in Jerusalem, in which he was "ravaging the church." Further on, in 9:1, he seeks formal collaboration from the high priest in Jerusalem to take action against Christians in Damascus. Regardless of particular problems that these descriptions raise in and of themselves, they do not jibe with Paul's testimony in Galatians 1:22–23 that he was "still unknown by sight to the churches of Judea . . ." and more particularly that those in Judea had only "heard it said, 'The one who formerly was persecuting us is now proclaiming the faith. . . .'" That is, though the Judean churches had heard the words of others regarding how Paul had persecuted them, the Judean church itself (so, at least, Paul's own remarks indicate) was not harassed or attacked by him.

Second, and consistent with the picture he paints in Philippians 3:3–8, Paul was "advanced in Judaism beyond many" and in particular "was far more zealous for the traditions of my ancestors." How good a student are you? Paul is better, more zealous, more advanced. Again, the language here is technical, as he refers to (one might literally translate) the "traditions of my parents." These "ancestors," or "fathers," or "parents" so named are, in the accepted parlance of the day, not meant to refer to one's particular family, but rather to the traditions of Torah study within Judaism (again, *Pirke Avot*, as discussed above; within the New Testament, for similar language see Mark 7:3 and Matt. 15:2). We can fill out this portrait, given Philippians 3:3–8, by recognizing a particularly Pharisaic or rabbinic element to Paul's study and training. More to the point (that Paul is making and building herein), he was not looking for any other tradition or sub-tradition but was content in excelling, within Judaism, within the traditions that he was studying.

Let us pause here and consider an interesting picture that is beginning to reveal itself. If we take Paul's many descriptions and passing references as pixels, perhaps he has given us enough already to begin to see an outline. It will be filled in more and more as the letter develops. Something is beginning to be clear: if indeed Paul was studied in, and zealous for, the law and if indeed these rival teachers, who appear to be *in some way* associated with the church in Jerusalem are somehow touting that law against Paul's gospel and if indeed their touting of the law is consistent with the Jerusalem church generally, then it might well make sense that Paul, as a persecutor, would not have persecuted the Jerusalem church. He (then), like them (then and now), was promoting "the law," or at least some particular take on it.

But something radical happened to Paul's understanding, approach, and agenda—something which he does not credit his training or experience up to that point. It didn't happen on Paul's time or via planning or effort on Paul's part. No. It happened when God "pleased" or "thought it seemly." The prominent place that that word, "pleased," takes in the sentence is basically impossible to reproduce in our vernacular. It would read something like this: "But when God pleased—that is, God who had set me apart from out of my mother's womb and who had called me through his grace—to reveal. . . ." Notice how the action of the whole sentence falls out from, and falls under, God and God's action in God's time.

The contrast with Paul's life to that point is clear: "But when . . ." The actor and originator are clear: "God." The timing is clear: "when God pleased . . ." The effecting element is clear: not human advancement or human training or the respected religious traditions in which Paul had been groomed, but "[God's] grace." Paul's calling was about God, and it was gifted by God to Paul. But was it a conversion?

Paul has clearly undergone a conversion of sorts, and one that we can with integrity label a "conversion" *if* we do not presume that it was a conversion out of Judaism. Why? Because it wasn't. That would have been impossible for Paul. At the time, Christianity was not a separate religion but a movement within Judaism. Paul remained a Jew, and his argument with the rival teachers is an argument with other Jews (who, like Paul, are also Christian) about how to proceed with welcoming Gentiles into the Christian movement. What is the problem with welcoming Gentiles into the Christian movement? The Christian movement is a movement *within*

Judaism—it proceeds, literally and figuratively, on Jewish terms. Paul and the rival teachers agree on that. They disagree about how to proceed. (For further discussion regarding the use of "conversion" with regard to Paul, see the Introduction to this volume.)

In the discussion above about the prophetic origins of the phrase "slave of Christ" (v.10), reference to Jeremiah (7:25) was made along with the statement that "loud echoes" of Jeremiah are heard in Galatians 1:15. That is certainly the case, and it has to do with Paul's description of himself as having been set apart by God "before I was born." Paul furthers his association with the prophets, and with Jeremiah in particular, with language that draws directly on Jeremiah's call narrative. Jeremiah 1:5 reads, "Before I formed you in the womb I knew you, and before you were born I consecrated you." Clearly Paul has drawn on that verse in presenting his (understanding of his) call.

The particular verb he chooses for "set apart" is not found in the Septuagint version of Jeremiah 1:5 and may or may not be Paul's own Greek translation of the Hebrew verb. It is, interestingly, the same word used in Acts 13:2 by the Holy Spirit to "set apart" Barnabas and Saul (Paul) for their first missionary journey. Perhaps more pertinent, it, like "slave of Christ," is clearly a term that Paul adopted with regard to himself, as evidenced in Romans 1:1: "Paul, a slave of Jesus Christ . . . set apart for the gospel . . . " (translation mine).

As dramatic as the notion of being "set apart" by God while still in utero is, what is perhaps (for Paul) the most telling part of the Jeremiah quotation is yet to come. He writes in verse 16 that God was pleased "to reveal his Son to me, so that I might proclaim him among the Gentiles." Again, the language of revelation is notable. We will get to that in a moment. But first, Jeremiah.

The final phrase in Jeremiah 1:5 reads, "I appointed you a prophet to the nations" or, one could also translate, "I appointed you a prophet to the Gentiles." The Greek word for "nations" as found in the Septuagint version of Jeremiah 1:5 is the same word Paul uses. In describing himself, and more importantly his mission, his "gospel," Paul is clearly drawing on Jeremiah. But there is more.

The language of apocalypse, or end times, as we have already observed, is evident in Galatians, not least in Paul's repeated use of "reveal"/"revelation." The term is not unknown in prophetic literature, and Paul may well be drawing on such passages as Isaiah 22:14, in which it states that God "revealed himself" to the prophet. But, striking as such a parallel is, it shares little or none of the context that Paul develops in Galatians.

The book of 2 Esdras, which was referenced above in the discussion of "the present evil age" (v. 4), shares with Paul an interest in apocalypse. Though perhaps written a few decades later than Galatians, the work draws on much of the same Jewish apocalyptic tradition that Paul does. In 2 Esdras 13:32–33, in a description of the end times, "The Most High" speaks to the prophet regarding "my Son [who] will be revealed" and references the "nations," or Gentiles, "[who] hear his voice." This is very much the scenario and context within which Paul finds himself and his mission. God has "revealed" to Paul God's "Son"—the very language Paul uses—and Paul is bringing that revelation to the "Gentiles" or nations.

Verse 16 ends, and verse 17 begins, with a restatement of what we already know from several statements beginning in verse 1: Paul's mission is not humanly ordained or authorized. Verse 17 begins the transition from "prehistory" to the history of the unfolding of Paul's missionary enterprise vis-à-vis other Christian enterprises and particularly that of the Jerusalem church. Jerusalem is named immediately in verse 17, setting up a series of descriptions in which it is named directly (1:18; 2:1) and indirectly (1:22–23, "Judea"; 2:11–12, via its representatives, "Cephas" and "certain people . . . from James"). Jerusalem, and particularly the Christian church based in Jerusalem, is literally (in the descriptions herein) and figuratively (via its influence) the central reference point as Paul unfolds his various movements on behalf of the gospel.

The mention of "those who were already apostles before me" perhaps also takes particular meaning in light of the mention of the Jerusalem church. In verses 18–19, the presumption is that James and Cephas are two "apostles" among others that Paul might have seen in Jerusalem. Similarly in 1 Corinthians 15:7, as the action unfolds in and around Jerusalem, the mention of "James . . . [and] all the apostles" suggests some number of individuals known as "apostles" based in Jerusalem (see similarly Acts 9:26–27). A precise definition, description, or delineation is nowhere given by Paul.

What does appear quite certain is that Paul's adoption of the title was disputed, at least in some circles. In 1 Corinthians 15:8, Paul seems to (humbly) relate himself to the other apostles by writing, "Last of all, as to one untimely born, [Christ] appeared also to me. For I am the least of the apostles, unfit to be called an apostle. . . ." Indeed, earlier in that same letter, he mounts an extended apology, or "defense," of his apostleship in response to those who examine or question or judge him (1 Cor. 9:2–3). There is likely a similar dynamic in Galatians, as Paul feels the heat to apologize for or explain his understanding of his apostolic mission in light of the (apostle-laden) Christian enterprise in Jerusalem.

The mention of both Arabia and Damascus are interesting taken singly and together. Notice that Paul says he *returned* to Damascus. Presumably, then, he started from there. So, in reconstructing this earliest part of Paul's travels following his call, we have a Damascus-Arabia-Damascus progression.

That first element of the pattern—the newly called Paul being present in Damascus—is consistent with the story of Paul's conversion as it unfolds in Acts 9. There Paul has significant contact with the already established Christian community in Damascus, where he "was baptized," "regained his strength," spent "several days" with the members of the community, and "began to proclaim Jesus" (Acts 9:18–20). Whatever happened at Damascus prior to Paul's departure (and eventual return), he downplays it by way of establishing his God-ordained, nonhumanly established mission.

The second part of the pattern, Paul's presence in Arabia and then Damascus, could be consistent with the story of Paul's escape from Damascus as told in 2 Corinthians 11:32–33 (cf. Acts 9:23–25). It is King Aretas (of the Nabatean kingdom of Arabia, to the east and south of Syria) who is after Paul and who receives the cooperation of the governor in Damascus to search for Paul. Whatever that king's concern with Paul might have been, we can surmise that it stems from some missionary activity of Paul's in Arabia. So, the story in 2 Corinthians appears to presume a time in Arabia followed by a stay in Damascus with both periods, again, being downplayed by Paul here.

5. Paul's Missionary Activity and First Jerusalem Visit
Galatians 1:18–24

1:18 **Then after three years I did go up to Jerusalem to visit Cephas and stayed with him fifteen days;** [19] **but I did not see any other apostle except James the Lord's brother.** [20] **In what I am writing to you, before God, I do not lie!** [21] **Then I went into the regions of Syria and Cilicia,** [22] **and I was still unknown by sight to the churches of Judea that are in Christ;** [23] **they only heard it said, "The one who formerly was persecuting us is now proclaiming the faith he once tried to destroy."** [24] **And they glorified God because of me.**

Paul's presentation of his call and the beginnings of his mission are more than simple remembrance. He writes with a purpose (countering the rival teachers, winning over the Galatians), and the elements of the story, as he tells it, are set out to serve that purpose. As already discussed, broad and specific strokes of this letter might be understood as apologetic; that is, as Paul defending himself against charges that have been lobbed. That sense is quite alive here, as Paul—even from a vernacular standpoint—goes on the defensive, saying at one point, "I do not lie!"

A TV news program that I occasionally watch begins something like this: "Our coverage begins . . . [short, dramatic pause] . . . now." The prominently placed adverb, "then," which occurs here and again at 2:1 (see also "But when," 2:11), has a similar affect. There is a strong downbeat. The story is unfolding, and it is leading—at the risk of giving a Wild West overlay to the drama—to a showdown.

"After three years," Paul tells us, he finally (?) ventures "up to Jerusalem to visit Cephas" and James. What has he been doing? He does not tell us. And for how long? The timeline is deceptively simple but leaves significant holes. For example, does "after three years" include the Arabian sojourn, or do the three years follow his return to Damascus from an unspecified length of time in Arabia? We don't know. Presumably, according to his call, he's been proclaiming his gospel message of God's "Son . . .

among the Gentiles" and presumably *that* is what prompts the trip, *and the expectation of such a trip*, to Jerusalem. Whom does he see?

Cephas will be familiar to readers of this volume from the Gospels and Acts as Peter, one of the Twelve who accompanied Jesus in his earthly ministry. "James the brother of our Lord," it is important to note, is *not* one of the Twelve (whose number did include two others named James) and does not figure in the Gospel accounts of Jesus' life and ministry as found in the New Testament (though he is named as Jesus' brother in Mark 6:3 and Matt. 13:55 and may, perhaps, be presumed present in the action of Mark 3:31–35, par. Matt. 12:46–50). First Corinthians 15:7 names him as an early witness of the resurrection and presumes his prominent role in the early church at Jerusalem. Acts 1:14 claims the presence of all Jesus' brothers from the earliest days of Christian assembly in Jerusalem, while Acts 1:15 appears to indicate that Peter was the first Christian leader there.

What the exact role of these two leaders, Peter and James, within the Jerusalem church might be, especially vis-à-vis each other, is unclear, though Acts 12:17 may suggest a viable answer: James remains on site, so to speak, while Peter is, with some regularity, out on mission trips. That is consistent with Paul's presentation of the two herein and, more broadly, with early Christian literature.

The particular verb that Paul employs here, "visit," is telling. It is notably nontechnical. It does not indicate or suggest any formal consultation, handing on or dispensing of information or knowledge, or teaching of any kind (cf. 1:12). Had someone or some group other than Paul conjectured or charged that Paul had at some previous time said that something more formal had occurred when he was in Jerusalem? Or had others argued or suggested based on other purported evidence that indeed something more formal had transpired? If so, Paul implies that they—not he—are to be discredited and disbelieved, because he is telling the truth.

Paul's language regarding lying is pointed and formulaic, and is somewhat muted in the NRSV translation. He very colorfully and dramatically states, "Behold, before God . . . I am not lying." This is the language of oath (cf. Rom. 1:9; 9:1; 1 Cor. 15:31; 2 Cor. 1:23; 11:31; 1 Thess. 2:5, 10; Phil. 1:8;). If one needs further proof (beyond the curses levied in 1:8 and 1:9) that Paul is dead serious in terms of his agenda and statements herein, then this oath helps to make the case.

Following the informal, friendly visit to Jerusalem, Paul writes, he furthered his missionary travels into Syria and Cilicia, the latter putting him in the area of his home city of Tarsus and getting fairly near to the Galatians themselves (to their southeast). As recorded in Acts, the first missionary journey of Barnabas and Paul (who begins the journey still being called "Saul") from Antioch (in Syria) to points west includes several locales within Cilicia (Acts 12:24–14:25). Following that account, within the extended narrative about the Jerusalem Council, Syria and Cilicia are named together in Acts 15:23 (which presumes Barnabas and Paul's activity there) and Acts 15:41, which records a second visit of Paul to the regions.

6. To the Heart of the Matter *and* to Jerusalem Again
Galatians 2:1–10

2:1 **Then after fourteen years I went up again to Jerusalem with Barnabas, taking Titus along with me.** [2] **I went up in response to a revelation. Then I laid before them (though only in a private meeting with the acknowledged leaders) the gospel that I proclaim among the Gentiles, in order to make sure that I was not running, or had not run, in vain.** [3] **But even Titus, who was with me, was not compelled to be circumcised, though he was a Greek.** [4] **But because of false believers secretly brought in, who slipped in to spy on the freedom we have in Christ Jesus, so that they might enslave us—** [5] **we did not submit to them even for a moment, so that the truth of the gospel might always remain with you.** [6] **And from those who were supposed to be acknowledged leaders (what they actually were makes no difference to me; God shows no partiality)—those leaders contributed nothing to me.** [7] **On the contrary, when they saw that I had been entrusted with the gospel for the uncircumcised, just as Peter had been entrusted with the gospel for the circumcised** [8] **(for he who worked through Peter making him an apostle to the circumcised also worked through me in sending me to the Gentiles),** [9] **and when James and Cephas and John, who were acknowledged pillars, recognized the grace that had been given to me, they gave to Barnabas and me the right hand of fellowship, agreeing that we should go to the Gentiles and they to the circumcised.** [10] **They asked only one thing, that we remember the poor, which was actually what I was eager to do.**

Perhaps the best known phrase of baseball great and famed wordsmith Yogi Berra is "it's déjà vu all over again." But he has many others, including, "yeah we're similar, but our similarities are different." One could hardly do better than to have the Hall of Famer introduce these next several lines of Paul's Letter to the Galatians. Here we go again: a trip to Jerusalem. And with a similar goal: to meet with revered Christian leaders. But is that similarity ever different (!), as Paul goes into important, one might even say excruciating, detail about this meeting. The stakes are high, and for the first time in the letter Paul gets to specifics. What is the core issue on which he and the rival teachers disagree?

A notable missing piece in Paul's recounting of his missionary activities thus far has been the lack of reference to any other name or group or base of operation. Certainly in comparison with the Acts accounts this stands out. There Damascus (arguably) and Antioch (clearly, 13:2) serve as bases of operation, providing support (human and material) for Paul's mission. Indeed, whether folks in and around that work would have considered it *Paul's* mission is itself a fair question to ask; throughout these chapters of Acts we consistently find listed "Barnabas and Saul" (12:25), that is Barnabas, the more prominent (?) and surely senior (in terms of time on the job) missionary being named first. Even within Paul's own letters we have noted at least the suggestion that Damascus served as a base of operation for a mission to Arabia (Gal. 1:17; 2 Cor. 11:32–33). More concretely, Paul regularly names coauthors and others who assist him. Why the silence? Were there really no colleagues, assistants, or sponsoring communities with whom Paul was associated up to this point?

The matter seems to be answered, perhaps a bit coyly, with the first sentence here: "I went up . . . with Barnabas and Titus. . . ." Now, that sounds more like the Paul we know (working with colleagues)! But still, what is left unstated and why?

Barnabas's presence here is telling. It confirms what we have presumed, that Paul has not been unaccompanied in his early missionary journeys. More so, it appears, at least, to confirm what is clear in the Acts accounts: Paul's early journeys are not solo enterprises but are part of a broader enterprise supported by the church at Antioch (where Barnabas is based). So, why keep that under wraps?

First, Paul consistently maintains the directly God-ordained nature of his mission. To get into detail regarding affiliations, such as that with the church at Antioch, would at least muddy the water, and at most raise suspicion, about his claim. Is his mission God-ordained or Antioch-ordained? If the listener is predisposed (by the rival teachers, for instance) to distrust missionary enterprises from churches other than Jerusalem and/or from Antioch in particular, then Antioch-ordained will not do.

Second, and more important, Paul writes at a time and from a place in which his missionary enterprise is indeed unaligned (with Antioch or any other church established before he began his work of establishing churches). That is in fact a God-ordained reality (for Paul, at least) at the present time and one that he is working to maintain and to further. He needs to paint for his listeners a picture of the development of *that* enterprise *in its relation to the church at Jerusalem*. So, that is what he does. Other matters (such as the history of the relationship of the Jerusalem and Antioch churches) are frankly, for him at the present time and in the present context of defending his position and winning over his Galatian listeners, beside the point.

Once we recognize that situation, all else falls into place. Titus is one that Paul was "taking along with" him, because—as we will see—Titus will serve as example par excellence to prove the merit of Paul's case; what his broader relationship to Paul *and* Barnabas or to their presumed dual missionary work in Syria and Cilicia (according to Acts) might have been is, again, immaterial for the development of Paul's argument. Paul "went up" to Jerusalem "in response to" the same (or a closely aligned and related) "revelation" from God, which has directed the entirety of his missionary enterprise because that enterprise is God-revealed. God has driven it from the first moment of Paul's calling which, we have little or no reason to doubt, was as dramatic (at least to and for Paul) as he relates. Paul "laid before them . . . the gospel that I [Paul; no need to reference Barnabas, Titus, or other colleagues here] proclaim among the Gentiles," because that was—and more importantly now *is*—the issue for Paul: his "gospel" mission "among the Gentiles."

Before moving even further into the heart of the matter, let us consider two matters. First, the particular verb that is translated in the NRSV as "laid before" is fairly technical and stands in stark contrast to the casual "visit" used for his first Jerusalem visit in 1:18. It is often used for formal disclosure or explanation before a recognized authority (see, e.g., 2 Macc. 3:9). It can also be used, somewhat less formally, for the sharing of information for consultative purposes (as in the Plutarch's [a contemporary of Paul's] *Moralia* 2.772d). Which is it here? And which does Paul suggest? Perhaps he is happy with the built-in ambiguity that the verb affords. Second, and even more interesting, is this phrase: "in order to make sure that I was not running, or had not run, in vain." Here Paul seems to be giving a very strong nod to the authority of the leadership with whom he was meeting. The suggestion is that their response would tilt the balance: if they approved, then he would know he was on the right course; if they disapproved, then he would (have to) recognize that his mission was misguided. Was that indeed his frame of mind going into the meeting? His firmly stated recognition of God's initial and ongoing role in directing his mission would suggest otherwise. Does that nod to human authority meet the needs of his presentation, here, in the Letter to the Galatians? Most certainly, as we are about to see.

With verse 3 we enter the heart of the matter. And it is a story told in two separable parts. First is the core issue, which is most easily followed by reading verse 3 and then jumping immediately to verses 7–9: "But even Titus . . . was not compelled to be circumcised, though he was a Greek"; indeed, the leadership extended "to me the right hand of fellowship, agreeing" that Paul's Gentile mission, with its no-circumcision policy toward Gentiles, was legitimate. Second, there is the story of the opposition or "false" leaders told in verses 4–6. These false leaders were working to undermine both Paul's mission and the "private meeting" (v. 2) which he and the Jerusalem authorities were enjoying with each other. We will briefly consider each part in order.

Whether Titus was literally "Greek" (i.e., from Greece) is not the concern. Here the term serves, precisely as it does in Galatians 3:28, in its relationship to "Jew"; that is, Titus is an uncircumcised non-Jew, or Gentile. He embodies the (very honest) tension raised by the expansion of the Christian movement to populations beyond Jews: to what degree should Gentiles who are welcomed into the Christian community be required to adapt to and adopt Jewish ways including, centrally, circumcision (the mark of all Jewish males)? The issue is a *Christian* one. That said, it is also a Jewish one insofar as most *Christians* (including the recognized Christian authorities in Jerusalem) are Jewish. What the matter decidedly is not is a Christian versus Jewish one.

At the risk of greatly oversimplifying the matter, and raising a host of other social, economic, and cultural issues, one might recall any number of Christian missionary movements in the nineteenth or twentieth century and to some degree in the twenty-first century. The movements were decidedly Christian; that is, they had to do centrally with expanding one or another Christian movement or, even more basically and centrally, with winning over converts to Christianity and establishing Christian communities in given locales. However, in comparing any one movement to any other, one could codify differences related to the particular ethnicity and culture from which the given movement had come: was a British or Belgian or German system of education presumed and variously demanded or provided? Were Western clothes invited or provided or demanded? Were "Christian" names demanded? Any one of these issues and more might quickly become contentious if a missionary leader were to step away from what had—up to that point—been practiced and expected, and started to institute a different practice—especially if the leader's reason for doing so went to the core of the movement itself: stating, for example, that the gospel itself called for such freedom from the given expected practice.

The Christian leadership in Jerusalem is Jewish, see themselves as Jewish, practice Judaism, and move within Jewish circles; they presume circumcision as a central mark of the individual's and the community's relationship with God. Paul stands before them with one who literally embodies his missionary enterprise: an uncircumcised, non-Jewish Christian. Will the Jerusalem leadership accept Titus and the movement he embodies? Yes! What about the opposition?

As Paul tells it, according to the NRSV alternative translation, the opposition is made up of "false brothers," or perhaps better, "false siblings" (see discussion of v. 2 above). This is important (and unfortunately lost in the primary NRSV translation) because it recalls all the kinship language already used and sets up that to come. These—and those whose positions and actions further their platform—are "false" and are not part of the family. That is interesting, because based on their promoting and (presumed) embodying of circumcision, they clearly bear the familiar marks of Judaism—see how complicated this is! Their presence is described as unwarranted and devious (they "slipped in to spy"), and, by extension, those who engage in furthering their platform now are similarly unwarranted. To make the point, Paul returns to a keynote he has already sounded and will continue to sound (see discussion on v. 4): slavery versus freedom.

It is not the Jerusalem authorities themselves who troubled Paul; it is, rather, those who are in some shadowy and unauthorized way connected with the Jerusalem church (v. 6) who caused Paul any pause. And they did proffer a real threat! But it was one that Paul was equal to on behalf of "the truth of the gospel."

The plasticity with which Paul variously uses and plays with the notions of one gospel or two (v. 7) is again evident in these verses. As noted above, it is perhaps the case that he himself remains somewhat unsettled on the matter (see comments on 1:6–7). In verse 5, *the* truth of *the* gospel is at stake—a statement made all the more strong when we recognize that only in this letter does he use this phrase, "the truth of the gospel," and he uses it twice (2:5 and 2:14). These two uses serve to underline the crucial relationship of the narrative of 2:1–10 and 2:11–14; further, they set up the contrasting statements regarding Paul himself (4:16) and the rival teachers (4:17; 5:7) later in the letter. That Peter, who is of course a recognized authority of the church at Jerusalem, is about to fall into Paul's bad graces (as told in 2:11–14) due to actions that Paul feels lack integrity (and go counter to the agreement in Jerusalem), has no bearing on the fact that Peter's broader "gospel" mission, whose object is "the circumcised," enjoys full integrity for Paul. What is interesting (and telling?) is that, as

Paul presents the matter, these are two separate gospels: one to the circumcised and one to the uncircumcised.

What is further telling is that, as this section draws to a close, Paul credits God (that is, "the one who worked through Peter" and also "through me") and not the church at Jerusalem for effecting both gospels. Perhaps here he betrays his bottom-line take on the matter and puts in further perspective the previous statements of verse 2 that suggest the mission-ordaining quality of the Jerusalem church's authority.

This section ends with a very suggestive statement regarding Paul's own (growing) agenda for his mission enterprise and his, and its, enduring relationship with the Jerusalem church. As indicated above in the introduction, Paul was to mount a deliberate and ongoing collection on behalf of "the poor" within the church at Jerusalem (Rom. 15:25–29, 1 Cor. 16:1–4, 2 Cor. 8–9). Interestingly, and as also noted in the introduction, Paul directly states in 1 Corinthians 16 that he has taken up the matter of that collection with the Galatian churches (in a lost second letter to them?). No discussion of the collection occurs in this letter, regardless of Paul's clearly stated enthusiasm for the task and its goal. That absence is perhaps further indication of the very pressing nature of Paul's twofold (countering the rival teachers; winning over the Galatians) goal here; nothing, not even the work of that collection, will draw him away from that goal.

"THE JERUSALEM COUNCIL" AND GALATIANS 2

As was discussed to some degree in the introduction, a crucial matter within scholarship on Paul is the manner in which the descriptions in Galatians, particularly those we've just considered in 2:1–10 and a bit more indirectly in 2:11–14, jibe with the descriptions of the Jerusalem Council in Acts 15. The matter is considered so important because it goes to the core of Paul's relationship with the Jerusalem church and has significant bearing on the chronology of Paul's mission and letters.

The scholarly discussion has as much to do with understanding the broad relationship of the Acts accounts with those in Paul's letters, as it does with a particular matter of the Jerusalem Council. Indeed, even the presumption that there was *one* Jerusalem Council that proceeded according to the account in Acts 15 is possibly undermined by Acts itself. What of Acts 18:22, which appears to indicate a formal (?), deliberative (?) meeting in Jerusalem following Paul's second (according to Acts) missionary journey? And perhaps even more telling—given the strength of the parallel with Galatians 2:10—what of Acts 11:27–30 regarding a meeting *in Antioch* involving a delegation from Jerusalem, which, interestingly, resolves that a collection be sent "by Barnabas and Saul" (that is, Paul) to the Jerusalem church? Does it bespeak yet another detail Paul has left out of the descriptions in Galatians 1 and 2 or another meeting?

However these questions may or may not be resolved, what is central to our consideration of Galatians is sorting out the situation within the churches to which Paul is writing and the way that Paul structures and makes meaning with his arguments. To that extent the Acts accounts are and have been (for the discussion of 2:1–10 above) vital without dominating our concerns. Our concern herein is the content and meaning of Galatians.

7. The Center Doesn't Hold (for Long)
Galatians 2:11–14

2:11 **But when Cephas came to Antioch, I opposed him to his face, because he stood self-condemned;** [12] **for until certain people came from James, he used to eat with the Gentiles. But after they came, he drew back and kept himself separate for fear of the circumcision faction.** [13] **And the other Jews joined him in this hypocrisy, so that even Barnabas was led astray by their hypocrisy.** [14] **But when I saw that they were not acting consistently with the truth of the gospel, I said to Cephas before them all, "If you, though a Jew, live like a Gentile and not like a Jew, how can you compel the Gentiles to live like Jews?"**

Any who have been involved, in the life of the church or in other contexts, with resolving conflicts and agreeing on terms of partnerships or non-competition clauses, only to see such resolutions or agreements—before too long—fail, will empathize with the action described within this section. Anyone who has been let down by a revered partner or colleague will too. Fair enough. But what about the following statement (which I mean to write from Peter's standpoint)? Anyone who gives a little extra to help smooth things over or to stake out a way forward, only to be harshly criticized for those good-faith efforts, will too. What are the complexities afoot in this section and how do they play out?

The words are strong, and the stakes are high. At the very least, the action herein, told from one side (wouldn't it be fascinating to hear Peter's side?), is indicative of growing pains of nascent Christianity. Agreements have been forged that make sense and allow for both the Jerusalem church and Paul to proceed with their enterprises and now, all of the sudden—following a period of particular goodwill in which Peter, the head of the "gospel for the circumcised" (2:7), associates directly and willfully with Gentile members of the church at Antioch—things backfire. What is going on?

48

From Paul's point of view what is going on stands in direct opposition to what has been agreed on. Further, it is "hypocrisy." As long as the broader Jerusalem delegation is absent, Peter seems to be having a good time of fellowship with all. "When in Rome do as the Romans," is a saying that suggests adopting the ways of those you are with; in Antioch, Peter appears to do as the Antiochenes. That is, he relaxes his observation of the Jewish laws of kashrut (kosher laws) and engages in table fellowship with Gentiles or some mix of Jews and Gentiles (consistent with the story of Peter and Cornelius in Acts 10, see esp. vv. 9–15 and 28). As soon as the colleagues from the Jerusalem church arrive (variously identified as "certain people from James" or "the circumcision faction," 2:12) Peter withdraws from contact with Gentiles (at least around meals) and resumes a more strict observance of kashrut. If we remember that James is the leader who stays put in Jerusalem and Peter is the one who goes out on missions (see discussion of 1:18–19, above) we might posit that these representatives of James are checking up on Peter and his activities. That would appear to be Paul's presumption.

From Peter's standpoint a number of things may have been in play—and been in play simultaneously: (1) he may indeed have been bending certain rules which he (and perhaps most of the Christian *and* non-Christian Jews with whom he associated) normally observed. (2) He may have been modeling a form of what we may call "situational ethics," in which one alters one's behavior, and expectations, based on the social context and individuals or groups involved; once the Jerusalemites had entered the scene (v. 12), he would (in similar fashion to how he changed his actions with and for the Antiochene Gentiles) make them welcome by recognizing their kashrut and expect others to follow suit. (3) He may have been swayed, however directly or indirectly, by the Jerusalem faction to recognize the importance of maintaining Jewish kashrut rules within Christian circles as a matter of policy—a policy that would not run contrary to the agreement of 2:1–10 since dietary laws were, by Paul's own testimony (or lack thereof), not addressed within that agreement.

However, and by whatever standards Peter acted, we can be relatively certain that he would not consider himself to be swayed by "hypocrisy" and likely intended to model Christian fellowship. One scenario to consider is that when colleagues from Jerusalem arrived, he sees a new and different situational opportunity to model fellowship. One might imagine Peter thinking, or even proposing, that it is time even for Paul himself, and the broader local leadership in this situation, to step up and observe the laws of kashrut (at least temporarily). After all, nobody—certainly not

Peter—calls into question the legitimacy of the agreement (recorded in 2:7) regarding uncircumcision. Rather, he acts with regard to another, apparently unresolved matter: table fellowship. In this case he acts in favor of recognizing the boundaries of Jewish kashrut (though precisely to what degree, we cannot say). If such a scenario approximates Peter's intentions, it was lost on Paul.

What may well have played out for Peter as a lost opportunity to display some understanding in two directions (first, he as head of the circumcision mission enjoying table fellowship according to Gentile norms with those of the uncircumsion mission; then, *vice versa*) plays out for Paul as not only hypocrisy but—and here's the rub—as a threat to what has already been decided. How dare Peter ask or suggest that Gentile Christians follow yet another set of Jewish rules (first there was the line in the sand around circumcision, now kashrut)! How dare he threaten the no-Gentile-circumcision agreement by trotting out kashrut! What will it be next? As a trained Pharisee, Paul was aware of a plethora of laws and areas of observance that one might proffer. And, he was willing to have none of it.

All "the other Jews" (including Barnabas, a hero of the uncircumcision mission) did, by Paul's testimony, go the way of Peter. Were they simply enjoying table fellowship (according to the familiar laws of kashrut) with each other? Were they modeling, or at least hoping to model, a particular form of Christian fellowship around kashrut, as suggested above? Were they indeed, as Paul accused, "hypocrites"? Regardless, the matter launches Paul into an extended statement about the nature and content of the Christian faith.

It is no coincidence that this incident happened in Antioch. The church of Jerusalem and the church of Antioch enjoyed an ongoing, if perhaps somewhat tense, relationship with each other. Paul was sponsored for a time, perhaps even trained, by and within Antioch's own missionary enterprise. Indeed, as noted above, Paul is, for his own purposes, likely downplaying in these verses the formal role that the church at Antioch itself played in launching the mission to the Gentiles/uncircumcised and in launching Paul, along with Barnabas, precisely on that mission. Antioch is a looming and important presence in and behind the scenes of the narratives of Paul's own mission enterprise and of mission to the Gentiles more broadly.

8. Faith, Law, the Gentile Mission, and Us
Galatians 2:15–21

2:15 We ourselves are Jews by birth and not Gentile sinners; ¹⁶ yet we know that a person is justified not by the works of the law but through faith in Jesus Christ. And we have come to believe in Christ Jesus, so that we might be justified by faith in Christ, and not by doing the works of the law, because no one will be justified by the works of the law. ¹⁷ But if, in our effort to be justified in Christ, we ourselves have been found to be sinners, is Christ then a servant of sin? Certainly not! ¹⁸ But if I build up again the very things that I once tore down, then I demonstrate that I am a transgressor. ¹⁹ For through the law I died to the law, so that I might live to God. I have been crucified with Christ; ²⁰ and it is no longer I who live, but it is Christ who lives in me. And the life I now live in the flesh I live by faith in the Son of God, who loved me and gave himself for me. ²¹ I do not nullify the grace of God; for if justification comes through the law, then Christ died for nothing.

This section follows directly on the heels of the previous one and may, indeed, simply be a direct continuation of it. The NRSV puts closing quotation marks after the last word of verse 14, and begins verse 15 without continuing the quotation marks, indicating that Paul has closed off the direct recounting of the incident at Antioch and has begun now to address his Galatian listeners directly. Some scholars, alternatively, consider the quoted response to Peter to continue through 2:21.

That the matter is ambiguous is not inconsistent with Paul's motives and goal. Clearly, the Antioch incident itself is recounted to exemplify the sorts of threats to, and reasons for, Paul's mission as it stands and the need for a letter such as this to defend and promote it. According to Paul's own description in verse 14, his words to Peter were meant to be heard by "all," and are certainly meant to be heard by his Galatian addressees now. Whether developed on the spot in Antioch or in composition of this letter, whether intended to be part of the original speech to Peter or an extension thereof for the Galatians, these words are presented as both called forth by the Antioch incident *and* as central to Paul's understanding of faith and mission as presented in the letter.

Given verse 15, with its direct appeal to a fellow Jew (i.e., Peter), the section may be best understood as having been structured as a continuing presentation of Paul's response to Peter.

That said, the placement and content of this section fall rather neatly into recognized rhetorical movements and categories of the time. According-ing to the *Rhetorica ad Herennium* 1:10.17, "when the statement of facts has been brought to an end, we ought first to make clear what we and our opponents agree upon . . . and what remains contested." Having closed out the statement of facts in 2:13 or 14, Paul would seem to continue in just such a manner, including both a statement of agreement (2:15) and a statement about that which is (at least for Paul) contested (2:16–21). Consistent with such an understanding, the NRSV treats this as a sepa-rate section.

We are now at the crux of the argument. In verse 16 Paul presents his understandings of justification, the action of God through Jesus Christ, faith, and the law. Fittingly, he does so via an inter-Jewish discussion.

The "we" beginning 2:15 clearly includes Paul and Peter and may include "all" the Christian Jews within earshot of them at Antioch. Though clearly the rhetorical force of the argument, as it is here situated within the letter, is meant for the Galatian addressees (and by extension all who would hear or read it), just as clearly, many (or most, or even all) of the Galatians would fall outside the pale of those who are "Jews by birth" (see introduction for the Gentile composition of the Galatian churches).

The parochial or elitist or boastful (see Rom. 3:27–28; 4:2) nature of 2:15 is not to be missed and beautifully sets up the arguments within the next verse and more broadly throughout the letter (see comments on 5:4, below). Paul begins from a familiar platform within and among those who consider themselves Jews. The easy congruence between "Gentile" and "sinner" is available within and around biblical tradition (Psalm 9:17, 1 Macc. 2:48) *and* is exemplified brilliantly within the New Testament by two different Gospel renderings of the same saying of Jesus: "Do not even the Gentiles do the same" (Matt. 5:47) and "For even sinners do the same" (Luke 6:33). Paul is talking insider to insider about those who are outside the pale: "Gentiles," "sinners."

He then moves onto another matter that "we" insiders clearly both "know," using a very broad and basic word for knowledge about God (Gal. 4:8) and other matters (Gal. 4:13). Here the "we," as will soon become clear, has been delimited. Gone, it would seem quite clear, are non-Christian Jews and particularly those non-Christian Jews who would have identified solely with the Pharisaic tradition that Paul knows so well (Gal. 1:14, Phil. 3:4b–6).

What Paul writes in 16b regarding "faith" and "Jesus Christ" would be hard for any Christian to argue with, and that indeed is the point. What Paul writes in 16a are fighting words, at least among Christian Jewish insiders. Here is where Paul begins to separate himself and his mission not just from the mission to the circumcised but also from what he perceives as a mindset that threatens the basis of the mission to the Gentiles.

Do works of the law justify? Virtually all who are associated with Lutheran, Reformed or Evangelical traditions would take that question as a touchstone for the crisis or question that each individual has to face for him/herself. That Protestant impulse has driven much that is good and interesting and definitive among various Christian traditions in Europe and America and elsewhere where such traditions have spread. But was that Protestant impulse Paul's purpose in raising the matter, or would he even have been aware of such an approach? Likely not.

The contrastive "yet" that begins verse 16 is telling. As it stands it marks a clear change in course or even, to use a driving metaphor, a grinding of the gears. Given verse 15, one would expect Paul to roll out one topic after another on which "we . . . Jews" would agree. But he does not. This "faith" statement stands in direct contrast to that which it immediately follows. So, in order to understand it, we need to understand that which immediately precedes.

That said, it is a complicating fact that this contrastive "yet," as we have it in the NRSV and in the Greek text on which the NRSV is based, is *not* present in the earliest manuscript witness to this text. Was it in the original text as Paul wrote it? There is significant manuscript evidence to indicate so, but we cannot be sure; its lack in the earliest manuscript witness we have is, to say the least, a nagging problem.

Regardless, Paul's emphatic use of a contrastive just prior to the phrase regarding "faith" and "Jesus Christ" enforces the same point. Rendered merely as "but" in the NRSV, that phrase might be more fully rendered into English as "but rather" or, even better, "except only." So, whether he indeed signals the contrast at the top of verse 16, as it stands in the NRSV, or only prior to the first "faith" statement, Paul is clearly setting apart that "faith" statement (and, by extension, the rest that follows) from the first full phrase in verse 16. It is to that phrase that we now turn in order to set the context for understanding the "faith" statement.

LAW DISORDERS

"A person is not justified by works of the law" or, perhaps better, as the Greek allows, "Humanity is not justified by the works of the law." Either rendering fits Paul's argument well. What he is countering—both within the letter itself and in the Antioch episode as it has just been rehearsed—is a position that reifies that something other than or in addition to "faith" justifies. What is that position?

Judaism? No. Paul's argument here is not with Judaism per se. Paul is arguing against a competing *Christian* position being forwarded by fellow Jews, who would uphold certain "works of the law" as necessary (at least Paul heard it that way) for justification. What might those "works of the law" be?

Several answers are possible, especially if we presume (wrongfully) that Paul is arguing willy-nilly against Judaism or Jews. But he is not. He is arguing against particular Christian Jews, and he is arguing for his particular understanding of Christianity and its implications, practical and otherwise, for Gentiles. Let's step back and ask, What have been the sources of tension thus far? Circumcision and dietary laws. Indeed, that is what Paul is speaking about when he raises "works of the law."

In current scholarship, there has been a slowly growing consensus over the past half-century around recognizing Paul's positions and argumentation herein, beginning with Krister Stendahl's groundbreaking article, "The Apostle Paul and the Introspective Conscience of the West," which seriously questioned the broadly Lutheran and Reformed presumptions that had set the agenda for reading this text. Currently many scholars, perhaps most prominently and forcefully James D. G. Dunn, are forwarding such an approach and are raising our understanding of the context and thrust of Paul's argument and the consequences thereof. What Paul is countering via the phraseology of "works of the law" are, in Dunn's words, "covenant works" or "identity markers," "not the law itself or law-keeping in general" (*Jesus, Paul, and the Law*, 191, 194, 200). Once such "covenant works"—food laws, for example—are raised to the level of "gospel" and rendered necessary for justification, then, argues Paul, "faith" loses its unique, central, and all-encompassing role, and Paul will have none of that. An immediate question for Christian leaders of any age to ask of themselves and their churches, in light of Paul's witness, is this: what "identity markers" or "covenant works" have we raised up, whether deliberately or inadvertently, that overshadow, or qualify, the "faith" about which Paul so forcefully speaks?

YA GOTTA HAVE FAITHFULNESS

As translated, "faith" (a noun) comes up twice in verse 16 and "believe" (a verb) once. In the Greek, the noun and verb forms are derived from the same root word, so the direct connection between them is clear. The question of how to translate the noun phrases is a vexed one, illustrated by the presence of the alternate readings in the NRSV: is the phrase best rendered "faith in Jesus Christ" (as favored within the NRSV text) or "the faith of Jesus Christ" (as given in the alternate readings)? Both can be seen as compatible with Paul's surrounding arguments and make some sense—especially when one understands the alternate to mean the *faithfulness* or even *trustworthiness* of Jesus Christ.

The verb phrase, which occurs immediately on the heels of the first noun phrase, is unambiguous on this point: "Christ Jesus" is the grammatical object of the verb, "believe" or, to be precise, of the preposition that follows the verb, rendering "we believed in Jesus Christ," or, as the NRSV has it, "we have come to believe in Jesus Christ." Now, there is some ambiguity or latitude in the meaning of the preposition "in," which, given the particular Greek preposition used, might be more accurately translated, "into" (see 3:27, "baptized into Christ," which translates this same Greek preposition).

Like the verb phrase, the noun phrase has its own parallels; indeed, far closer ones. In Romans 3:3 Paul refers to "the faithfulness of God" while in the same letter, in 4:16, he writes of "the faith of Abraham" (see similarly Rom. 4:12). Indeed, common Greek usage clearly favors this rendering of the phrase with the subjective, as opposed to the objective, genitive; that is, "faithfulness of Christ" over "faith in Christ." And though Paul might have forwarded his own, somewhat idiosyncratic, sense of the phrase in his direct teaching and preaching, it is noteworthy that the phrase comes up also in the Letter to the Romans, a community that did not know him personally or have the benefit of any personal engagement with his teaching or preaching. Consistent with the common Greek usage, they would have heard "faithfulness of Christ" (Rom. 3:22, 26) just as they would have heard "faithfulness" of God or of Abraham in those other surrounding verses.

Given all of that, rendering our verse according to common Greek usage would seem to make good and interesting sense of Paul's usage:

We know that humanity is not justified through works of the law but only through the faithfulness of Jesus Christ. And we believed into Jesus Christ

in order that we might be justified through the faithfulness of Jesus Christ
and not through works of the law. . . .

Notice what has happened in this translation vis-à-vis that of the
NRSV. There, three virtually synonymous and relatively flat phrases
occur in a row: "faith in Christ . . . believe in Christ . . . faith in Christ."
Each of the three indicates an act of faith or believing in a grammatical
object (Christ) and none of the three indicates much, or anything, else.
In the translation above, which takes Paul's own language at face value
and in the context of surrounding arguments, a colorful and suggestive
verb phrase indicating faithful participation into, or (ethical and/or mystical) engagement with, Christ is bookended by parallel noun phrases
that describe Jesus Christ's own ongoing faithfulness. Christ both models
(Phil. 2:1–11) and enacts (Rom. 3:21–26) that which justifies, while the
believer participates in, or "into," Christ (see Gal. 3:20, 27; 4:9; Rom.
6:4–5). Now that sounds like Paul!

A very telling allusion to Psalm 143 closes out this verse. Psalm 143:2
reads, "for no one living is righteous [or, "justified"] before you." Through
his modification of that verse, Paul begins to set up two broad and important platforms for argumentation to which he will return. The first has to
do with "flesh." The NRSV shortchanges Paul's language with its simple
translation, "no one"; what Paul writes is "all flesh." That is a somewhat
striking phrase in itself, and perhaps more importantly is one that uses a
term and a complex concept, "flesh," to which Paul will return repeatedly
in the letter (2:20, 3:3, 4:23, 29, 5:16, 17, 19, 24, 6:8, 12, 13; for a handy
discussion of the term and its use in other letters, esp. Romans, see comments on 5:16). Among other things, the use of "flesh" points the listener
in the direction of the time-honored practice of circumcision, which does
not, in and of itself, participate in "the Spirit" (again, see further discussion
in comments on 5:16). Second, Paul is positing that "works of law" (such
as circumcision and dietary restrictions) are ineffective and not necessary
for Gentile converts, since it is not through such that they are justified.

Another notable term and complex concept that Paul uses here is "justified." As indicated in the citation from Psalm 143 indicated above, "justified" and "righteous" are two English translations of the same Greek root
word. To be justified is to be or become "righteous" before God. We know
that Paul credits Christ, and Christ's faithfulness (2:16) with effecting
the justification or righteousness of humanity. To have faith, or practice
faithfulness, "into" Christ (again, see discussion above), is the appropriate response and the touchstone of living within Christian community.

Anything else is, at best, an add-on and at worst misleading. Paul would put his rivals' promoting of "works of law" in the latter category—misleading, and therefore threatening to Paul's "gospel" message regarding God's action through Christ.

IT'S PERSONAL

As Paul moves toward the climax of this section, where he puts the final points on his central argument (vv. 20–21), he steps back to appeal to his own personal experience in verses 17–19. Remember, his presumed inter-locutors throughout this section (including, via the "we," vv. 15–21), Peter and "all" who are engaged at Antioch, share Paul's Jewish experience with the law and, we know and they know, have at the very least been promot-ing the stipulation of dietary "laws" even for uncircumcised, non-Jewish Christians and may have, directly or indirectly, threatened to (re)invoke the necessity of circumcision.

Verse 18 anchors this subsection as Paul hypothetically (via the "if") and paradigmatically puts himself in the place of a Christian leader who would reinstate such laws as circumcision and dietary restrictions. That is, Paul's "I" here stands for Christian leadership at the early and crucial moment in the movement's history. Clearly the move considered here is for Paul wrong and necessarily leads to becoming a "transgressor," which is, ironically and coincidentally, a synonym for those presumed outsiders, the Gentile "sinners" of verse 15, as is indicated in this verse from that New Testament letter that has James's name attached to it: "But if you show partiality, you commit sin and are convicted by the law as transgres-sors" (Jas. 2:9). Not that the right course necessarily leads to success (v. 17), but it does put dietary and circumcision laws in proper Christian perspec-tive and does open one up to the promises of God through Christ (v. 19).

The colorful and striking language of dying and living in verse 19 is similar to that found elsewhere in Paul's letters, both those following (Rom. 6:8, 10–11; 2 Cor. 13:4, Phil. 3:10) and preceding (1 Thess. 5:10) the writing of Galatians. The subjunctive mood, the "might"-ness, that pops up in the middle of verse 19 is telling and sets up well what is coming in the close of verse 19 through verse 20.

Christ has been crucified (and resurrected) and, more to the point, the paradigmatic "I"—which stands for all Christians—has "been cru-cified with Christ." That is a given, if a complicated given—one which goes to the heart of Paul's understanding of both salvation and of ethics.

Remember verse 16? It is about Christ—particularly Christ's faithfulness
and believing "into" Christ's faithfulness—and not about adding or sup-
plementing with one or another "identity markers" such as circumcision
or food laws or _____ (fill in the blank with whatever marker[s]
your tradition might demand).

The first part of verse 20 takes us directly into the realm of ethics;
that is, how individuals and communities "live." The passing reference to
"flesh," as we have already seen by the addition of "flesh" to Psalm 143:2
as alluded to in verse 16, is no mistake but quite deliberate. Paul, and
Paul's model Christian—the "I"—lives "now . . . in the flesh . . . by faith
in the Son of God" without any fleshly markers such as circumcision or,
by extension, food laws.

The complications within verse 20 are similar to those with the noun
phrase "faith in Christ"/"faithfulness of Christ" in verse 16. However,
verse 20, as a whole, is just a bit more drawn out and more complicated.
Consistent with its ethical basis, it references living "in faith" or living
"by faith." The second, instrumental sense, living "by," is that which is
adopted by the NRSV and with good reason—though the simple Greek
preposition for "in" is used here, that same preposition can, and often
does, indicate the "instrumental" sense: that is, how something is accomplished. Since Paul is here talking about how, not where, living occurs, the
NRSV's "by" makes good sense.

The second "in" is the problematic one in the NRSV, along the same
lines as it is in verse 16. Assuming the same common Greek usage as we did
in verse 16, this verse becomes "and it is no longer I who live, but living in
me is Christ. What is now living in the flesh, lives by the faithfulness of the
Son of God, who loved me and gave himself for me." The use of "faithfulness" and the recognition of the subjective genitive—that it is "faithfulness," which has the Son of God as its subject or source and not "faith,"
which has the Son of God as its object—make perfect sense and put the
final phrase and the whole verse in proper perspective. It is all about "Christ
. . . the son of God." That final phrase "loved me and gave himself for me"
spells out Christ's salvific (cf. Rom. 6) and ethical (cf. Phil. 2) action; it indicates what Christ's "faithfulness" resulted in: salvation for all. (Paul's "me"
is, again, the paradigmatic "I," which stands for all Christians.)

The section ends by putting an exclamation point on Paul's overrid-
ing and undergirding understanding that it is God—not solely or in any
limited way Christ alone—who is the source of grace and salvation and
the foundation of faith (Gal. 3:6; cf. Rom. 4:3, 5; 1 Thess. 1:8). And that
is an important point for Christian readers today to grasp, for there is no

Christian monopoly on grace. Paul knew that, of course, as he was arguing for a particular and overarching understanding of grace for his Galatian addressees over and against, and in light of, notions of grace resonant with his fellow (Christian) Jewish interlocutors.

There is nothing anti-grace about Judaism, as a quick glance at the biblical tradition, let alone other ancient writings, indicates (see comments on 1:6, above). Paul's rivals for the Galatians' attention, it might well be presumed, felt themselves to be forwarding God's grace. Indeed it may well be those very rivals who painted Paul as one who would "nullify God's grace." Paul turns them and (if we allow him) us on their/our heads. Far be it from the Christian individual or community to set up anything other than, or separate from, Christ's "faithfulness" to live by or through! To do so would be to "nullify the grace of God."

9. Right Back at You
Galatians 3:1–5

3:1 **You foolish Galatians! Who has bewitched you? It was before your eyes that Jesus Christ was publicly exhibited as crucified. ² The only thing I want to learn from you is this: Did you receive the Spirit by doing the works of the law or by believing what you have heard? ³ Are you so foolish? Having started with the Spirit, are you now ending with the flesh? ⁴ Did you experience so much for nothing?—if it really was for nothing. ⁵ Well then, does God supply you with the Spirit and work miracles among you by your doing the works of the law, or by your believing what you heard?**

Throughout 2:11–21, and particularly 2:14 and what follows in 2:15–21, Paul's addressees have been listening in on a previous argument. Now Paul takes the complex set of circumstances, arguments, and counterarguments that would define Christian mission for his time and arguably all time directly to the Galatians. The previous section, as we saw, lays out what is contested. This section sets out to argue for and prove the position Paul stakes out. And he begins by recalling, with some attitude, the very teachings with which he founded the Galatian churches. Though calling one's addressees foolish, then as now, has some sting, it is probably the particular context of conversion or training that Paul is bringing in and wants his addressees to hear. Within the New Testament this is best exemplified in Titus, chapter 3: "for we ourselves were once foolish" (v. 3) way back when, before "God our Savior" (v. 4) "saved" (v. 5) us. Indeed, that whole chapter and section of Titus begins with the directive, "Remind them"; that is, remind your listeners of who they are as "saved ones." That is what Paul is doing here.

The Galatians are "foolish" because they have reverted to their preconversion, pre-Christian ways. That is itself somewhat ironic, since Paul's grievance with them is that they have entertained and are being swayed by teachers who are promoting the practice of Jewish laws among these

largely or exclusively non-Jewish, uncircumcised believers. For the Galatian Christians and for their current teachers, these Gentile converts are
probably maturing *further into* their *Jewish* Christian life. But Paul says no.

The language of verse 1b is perhaps both pointed and somewhat loose.
Paul is at least indirectly, through the use of "bewitched," accusing them
of succumbing to magic or superstition. At the same time, the term had
for centuries been used to characterize other, usually rival, teachers and
their ability to sway others "with smoke and mirrors," we might say by an
approximation in an English idiom. Clearly, Paul is indicating his lack of
respect for those whose teachings are winning over the Galatians.

The last part of the verse is somewhat of a restatement of 2:16 and
begins to fill in some of the blanks that Paul suggests in his statement
about Christ's faithfulness. That faithfulness manifested itself in crucifixion (see esp. Phil. 2:8, which is part of the so-called Christ Hymn of Phil.
2:5–11).

Beyond the Christ Hymn, this passage resonates with Paul's summary
teachings about Christ, such as 1 Corinthians 1:23 and 2:2 and, in this letter, Galatians 5:11 and 6:12. It is precisely this story of "Christ crucified"
(to quote 1 Corinthians 1:23), its content and effects, that Paul "publicly
exhibited" when he founded the Galatian Christian community, and it is
upon this and this only that the community should stand.

Now, in verse 2, Paul introduces language that heretofore in the letter
has been missing. The reasons for bringing in the Spirit here, and its role
within both the rivalry between Paul and his opponents and within the life
of the Galatian churches, are something of a mystery. Does Paul introduce
it in response to his rivals' teachings about, and experience of, the Spirit
(so Martyn) or as a manner of recalling for the Galatians their own past
experience with the Spirit (so Betz)? Of course, these two choices need
not be mutually exclusive. That said, on balance I favor the latter for two
reasons: (1) Paul's entrée into this section recalls the Galatians to their
initial conversion under his teaching; and (2) the prevalence, depth, and
breadth of "Spirit" language not only throughout this letter (4:6; 5:16)
but throughout other of Paul's letters from the earliest to the last suggest
strongly that it was in fact a basic element of his teaching and presentation
(Rom. 8:2, 11; 1 Cor. 2:12; 3:16; 6:19; 15:45; 1 Thess. 4:8).

The contrast in 3:2 parallels that in 2:16: "works of the law" over and
against believing in Christ (2:16) or "what you have heard" (that is, what
they received through Paul's initial missionary preaching to them, 3:2).
Interestingly, the label given the reception of that hearing is "the Spirit."
Restated in verse 3 is the motif of foolishness, which marks a return to

their preconversion state, as we saw in the remarks above regarding verse 1. And, to emphasize that, Paul reminds them that they "started with the Spirit" (see similarly 4:6) and, by implication, would do well to stick with the Spirit (see esp. 5:16–18, 25). Indeed, it is more than implication as Paul contrasts "Spirit" with "flesh"—his first attempt at providing descriptive content for what the Spirit is or entails, in this case via the negative statement of what the Spirit is not—that is, "flesh." And Paul has already stated what flesh is and is subject to: "all flesh" (2:16; though as noted above, it is not evident in the NRSV translation, "no one") will *not* "be justified by works of the law."

Following the bridge of verse 4, which raises the unthinkable eventuality that the Galatians will indeed turn their backs on Paul, the Spirit, and gospel that Paul preached and that "the Spirit" defines or delimits (v. 2), Paul provides an expansive and colorful sentence, which both summarizes what has been said and sets a foundation for what is coming. God's action is ongoing, in the most basic grammatical and the most profound theological sense, as is indicated by the use of two present active participles—"supplying" and "effecting"—which are translated too plainly in the NRSV as "supply" and "work." Paul writes, "God [continually] is supplying the Spirit and [continually] is effecting miracles among you. . . ."

To close out this section Paul poses a loaded question. Regarding God's continuing action of supplying the Spirit and effecting miracles I ask you now, O foolish Galatians (one can almost hear Paul repeating), does all of that come your way "through works of the law or through the hearing of faith (or proclamation of faith)?" Do you think it is about adopting circumcision and dietary laws or about relying on or, perhaps better, relying "into" (see discussion of 2:16, above) God's action through Jesus Christ? Clearly Paul knows the answer and just as clearly—or so he hopes—they will too, once he is able to seize a lynchpin of the rivals' argument for the Galatians' attention and convince the Galatians of their full status (already)—they need not adopt the practices of the rival teachers.

10. Descendants and Heirs
Galatians 3:6–4:7

This long section is made up of several important, distinct discussions, familiar for their imagery and basic content. As is indicated in the paragraph structure of the NRSV translation, these include Abraham's faithfulness, 3:6–9; law and curse, 3:10–14; Abrahamic promise and inheritance, 3:15–19; "Why then the law?" 3:19–25; faith, baptism, and inheritance, 3:26–29; and slavery, freedom, adoption, and inheritance, 4:1–7. Though each of these and the matters they raise have spawned book-length treatments in their own right, their immediate purpose in the letter is very closely intertwined with each other and with the immediate context on either side of this broad and deep section of the letter. Indeed, by way of a simple exercise, skip this section for a moment by reading 3:1–5 immediately followed by 4:8–11. Notice the relative ease with which the two sections work together, particularly their congruity of content (abandoning of Paul's gospel message and teaching) and tone (shock and frustration: "Are you so foolish," 3:3; "How can you . . . ?" 4:9).

So, should readers of this great letter skip this great section, 3:6–4:7? To quote Paul from another letter, "Let it not be so!" Rather, when engaging the particular arguments within this section readers ought to do so without losing sight of its coordinated function *as a discrete section* of the letter and of how the subsections and arguments work together to support, bolster, and forward Paul's plea: "we" (that itself is a word we want to look at closely in the section) are all children and heirs of God's promise.

ABRAHAM: FATHER OF FAITH
Galatians 3:6–9

3:6 Just as Abraham "believed God, and it was reckoned to him as righteousness," [7] so, you see, those who believe are the descendants of Abraham.

[8] And the scripture, foreseeing that God would justify the Gentiles by faith, declared the gospel beforehand to Abraham, saying, "All the Gentiles shall be blessed in you." [9] For this reason, those who believe are blessed with Abraham who believed.

One wonders whether Paul was looking forward to or dreading this point in his presentation. As every (Jewish) schoolchild then knew, and certainly every teacher of Jewish traditions, "Abraham was the great father of a multitude of nations, and no one has been found like him in glory. He kept the law of the Most High and entered into a covenant with him; he certified the covenant in his flesh." So begins the section on Abraham in the closing chapters of Sirach (44:19–20), which consider, one after another, several pillars from Scripture and Israel's history. Though written about two hundred years prior to Galatians, Sirach is a product of the Hellenistic era and provides a good approximation of the place and understanding of Abraham within Judaism at the time. As with Washington or Lincoln in political debates within the United States, or Luther or Calvin in debates among Protestants, Abraham is one to invoke to bolster a position. That is especially the case, as is likely here, if the other side has already done so. But how was Paul to bring Abraham, who underwent circumcision as a sign of his own conversion, over to Paul's side of the debate?

The very next line in Sirach provides something of a clue: ". . . when [Abraham] was tested he proved faithful" (see also 1 Macc. 2:52). And so Paul approaches Abraham. The simple but telling "Just as," which is one word in Greek, ties Abraham directly to the previous verse and, particularly, the last part of the previous verse—faith or, as in the NRSV, "believing." Abraham, the great model, acted "just so," and so should "you."

Similarly, the next verse begins with simple, strong language. The NRSV has "so, you see . . ." In fact, the verb Paul uses is a standard word for "know," and its usage here, though ambiguous, is strong. It may represent either the simple present, "so you know now," or perhaps more likely the imperative, "know now. . . ." Either way—stating the (hoped-for) influence and result of his argument up to this point or presenting a command—Paul's pointed use of "know" and "now" indicate in no uncertain terms that he is locked in a competition for the shape of the young church at Galatia. To state the obvious by way of extending the metaphor, having Abraham and Abraham's legacy on your side is a crucial and definitive prize in determining the outcome of that competition.

In a later time and another place, Paul again treated Abraham in an extended manner, in the fourth chapter of Romans. A brief comparison of our verse here with Romans 4:16–17 reveals something about Paul's varying agenda: "For this reason it depends on faith, in order that the promise . . . may be guaranteed to all his descendants, not only to the adherents of the law but also to those who share the faith of Abraham (for he is the father of all of us, as it is written, 'I have made you the father of many nations'). . . ." In Galatians 3 there is no such apparent breadth to Paul's message or purpose regarding Abraham. Paul is here countering certain "adherents of the law" who are strongly suggesting or demanding that Gentile believers—who by definition are nonadherents of the law— become adherents. This is not the occasion for a broader consideration of "all" of Abraham's "descendants." Interestingly, the broad umbrella that Paul constructs in Romans 4:16–17 may not be inconsistent with the Paul of Galatians 3 (indeed, he very likely would include himself among adherents of the law), but his purpose and focus here is to counter and cut off the influence of the rival teachers.

Within a few verses, Paul will use a particular term for Abraham's descendants or "offspring," literally "seed" (Gal. 3:16). As we will see, Paul will make a lot of that word in developing his understanding of Christ. And that is the same word that Paul uses repeatedly in Romans 4 (and Rom. 9:7–8) where it is consistently, and confusingly vis-à-vis this chapter of Galatians, translated by NRSV as "descendants." Here, the word translated "descendants" means, literally, "sons," or "children." Given that nowhere else in his letters does Paul use the phrase, "children of Abraham," and that within a few verses he switches to "seed" (consistent with his treatment of Abraham in Romans), it appears very likely that in invoking "children of Abraham" here Paul is taking over a central plank of the opposing teachers' platform and turning it against them.

Finally vis-à-vis Romans 4:16–17 it is worthy of note that within the NRSV, "nations" in Romans and "Gentiles" herein are translations of the same Greek word. Though it would be helpful, in order to show consistency within Paul's own language, to use one or the other term in both Romans and Galatians, the choices of the NRSV translators are fitting to the given contexts of each letter. Here in Galatians the issue is simply and profoundly how to bring Gentiles into the Christian fold and how to counter the opposing teachers' platform for doing so.

Verse 8 unfolds tellingly and deliberately according to Paul's design. He has already quoted Genesis 15:6 regarding how Abraham "believed." Just prior to that verse in Genesis is the famous narrative of God's demonstration to Abraham that, as are the stars of heaven, "so," says God, "shall your descendants be." Traditionally understood, those descendants are the Jewish nation. Indeed, it is that promise that Abraham "believed" and it is that promise so understood regarding the Jewish nation that the opposing teachers would likely have highlighted with regard to this verse in building their case for the Gentile Christian practice of circumcision according to Jewish law.

Paul, of course, has other ideas. He has clearly distinguished faith from law in verse 5. Now he frames the following citation in succinct and focused language regarding Scripture: it foresaw that "God would justify the Gentiles by faith." Following Paul's argument thus far, his hearers know what faith is and is not, and it is not the establishing of Jewish law among Gentiles. It has to do with Christ and Christ's faithfulness, and believing in (or "into") that (see above comments on 2:16).

Further, and interestingly, according to Paul, Abraham stands as a proto-witness of, or model for, the gospel of Jesus Christ. First, Scripture "declared the gospel beforehand" to Abraham. The compound verb "to declare the gospel beforehand" is used only here within the letters of Paul and, more broadly, the New Testament. It fits Paul's purposes well here as he finds and defines the basis for his own gospel (see 1:6–7, 8). Of course the term's very uniqueness also raises the question of whether the teachers might have used this term or the similar phraseology regarding the "foreseeing" activity of Scripture. Such usage that renders "Scripture" as a kind of actor or agent capable of (fore)seeing and other activities is known in the Jewish—including rabbinic—literature of Paul's time and resonates with Paul's usage elsewhere in Galatians (Gal. 3:22, "imprison," and 4:30, "say"; for several other instances of "say," see Rom. 4:3; 9:17; 10:11; 11:2).

Given such a dramatic setup, it is interesting that the quotation here is actually not precisely extant in any known ancient version of this scriptural text. Most often cited are Genesis 12:3; 18:18; and 22:18. It is Genesis 18:18 that according to the text in the Septuagint (widely circulating in Jewish and, later, Christian circles in the immediate centuries before and after Christ) matches Paul's citation most closely (with the exception of reading "in him" for Paul's "in you"). It is easy to see how Genesis 22:18 may well be looming in the background, because it is regarding Abraham's "seed."

Why did God, or Scripture, act in such a way regarding Abraham? "For this reason," or more simply "so that," "those [who are justified] by faith are being blessed with faithful Abraham." As in 2:16, so here: Paul favors the noun to the verb form of "faith." For that reason the "faith" part of verse 8, "God would justify the Gentiles *by faith*," is paralleled directly in verse 9, which reads literally "those *by faith*" where the NRSV has "those who believe." And consistent with not using verbal forms, Paul does not use a verb form with regard to Abraham either. Simply put and consistent with the Sirach text cited above, *Abraham is "faithful."*

THE LAW, THE CURSE, CHRIST, AND ABRAHAM
Galatians 3:10–18

3:10 **For all who rely on the works of the law are under a curse; for it is written, "Cursed is everyone who does not observe and obey all the things written in the book of the law."** [11] **Now it is evident that no one is justified before God by the law; for "The one who is righteous will live by faith."** [12] **But the law does not rest on faith; on the contrary, "whoever does the works of the law will live by them."** [13] **Christ redeemed us from the curse of the law by becoming a curse for us—for it is written, "Cursed is everyone who hangs on a tree"—** [14] **in order that in Christ Jesus the blessing of Abraham might come to the Gentiles, so that we might receive the promise of the Spirit through faith.**

[15] **Brothers and sisters, I give an example from daily life: once a person's will has been ratified, no one adds to it or annuls it.** [16] **Now the promises were made to Abraham and to his offspring; it does not say, "And to offsprings," as of many; but it says, "And to your offspring," that is, to one person, who is Christ.** [17] **My point is this: the law, which came four hundred thirty years later, does not annul a covenant previously ratified by God, so as to nullify the promise.** [18] **For if the inheritance comes from the law, it no longer comes from the promise; but God granted it to Abraham through promise.**

Paul's argument takes a turn here. Or does it? Consideration of Abraham and his "offspring" will return in verse 14 and 15–18. Meanwhile, this section is connected with the previous both by the simple conjunction, "for," and by a parallel identifying the subject of verse 10, which sets up the discussion and explanation to follow, with the subject of verse 9. More broadly, Abraham and the preached-beforehand gospel firmly set the context and goal of these verses, which is addressed directly to the Gentile Galatians regarding their inclusion as children and heirs of God's promise to Abraham and through Christ.

Beyond the use of the conjunction "for," which forwards the content of verse 9, Paul further signals direct connections with the previous verse. He sticks with his labels for the differing camps: "the ones by faith" of verse 9 are here contrasted by, literally, "those by the works of the law." Further, consistent with verses 7–8, Paul here provides an explanation or result of scriptural interpretation previous to providing the scriptural warrant. In so doing, he introduces the language of "curse."

This is a different word for curse than used at the top of the letter in Galatians 1:8–9 and reflects the text under consideration, Deuteronomy 27:26 (according to the Septuagint version). Nowhere else, besides here and verse 13, is this word found in Paul's letters. The phrase, "under a curse," resonates with other phrases Paul will use as the letter continues to unfold, most directly "under the power of sin" (3:22) and "under tutors and guardians" (4:2), and "enslaved to [literally, "under"] the elemental spirits of the world" (4:3).

Also consistent with the citation in verse 8, Paul's quotation here does not match exactly any extant ancient text of the Scripture cited. That said, he is clearly drawing on Deuteronomy 27:26, which would seem to prove precisely the opposite of what Paul takes it to affirm. What is going on here? Whether any given individual or group is on the positive side (obeyed "all things written in the book of the law") or negative side (have not done so) of the ledger, "all" are operating "under the curse." That is how and why the matter is ritualized in and around Paul's base text, Deuteronomy 27:26 (see, more broadly, 27:1–26) wherein "all the people say, Amen" to the curse.

With that understanding in place, Paul's decidedly compact and seemingly complex mode of citation and argumentation here falls into place. Would or should Paul's (Gentile) addressees in Galatia deign to enter into the arrangement between God and Israel, dramatically ritualized under Moses' leadership in a ceremony organized around a series of curses, as told in chapter 27 of the book of Deuteronomy? To put it mildly, Paul thinks not. And the next two in this compact series of verse citations bolster and refine Paul's position.

In the introductory section of verse 11, Paul again provides the learning derived from the given base text before citing the text itself. Taken from Habakkuk 2:4, though—consistent with earlier citations—not precisely matching other known versions of the text, the citation reads, "The one who is righteous will live by faith." An alternative reading provided within the NRSV is equally compelling, "The one who is righteous by faith will live." It is difficult to determine which one Paul might have favored. The pattern that Paul builds in the parallel constructions within verses 9–10 using "by faith," suggests favoring the alternative reading; that the one who is righteous by faith will live.

Either way, the direct parallel of the phraseology of "by faith" provides the key to, and colors, the whole argument. From the first book of the Bible and the traditional father of the faith, it is clear that those who are "by faith" are those for whom the gospel was prepreached (verse 8) and for whom it is being preached now. Further, as Paul's addressees would have known and heard, the word for "righteous" and "justified" share the same root (see comments on 2:16, above). That, in turn, would draw them a bit further back in the letter, to recall 2:16; it is faith and not law by which "a person is justified." Here, the prophet affirms that it is faith, and not law, that brings life. Similarly verse 9 regards the story of Abraham. From the standpoint of Scripture, then, in these few verses Paul has shown (or, meant to anyway) that both the Law (i.e., the Torah or first five books of the Bible) and the prophets affirm his "gospel."

The introductory section of verse 12 maintains the practice of precitation summation. Consistent with Paul's compact phraseology regarding "faith" to this point and inconsistent with the NRSV translation, Paul writes simply that "the law is not by faith" and goes on to quote part of Leviticus 18:5. Given the understanding and approach that Paul has established, and the introduction he has provided, *and* in light of his citation of Deuteronomy 27:26, the statement of Leviticus 18:5 appears fairly evident and even redundant. Of course those who are "by the law" (v. 10) live by the law and under the curse agreement of Deuteronomy 27 and therefore, within this argument, not by faith. Interesting to note is Paul's use of the future tense (which Paul inherits from his base text—Lev. 18:5 according to the Septuagint). It helps to reinforce Paul's broader argument that his addressees have a choice, and there are consequences to the choice they make: do they wish to choose that gospel that Paul preached and live by or "into" (2:16) Christ, or do they want to (give that up and) live by "them," that is, Jewish laws?

It is with verse 13 that Paul moves his argument forward by reintroducing the theme of "curse" and bringing Christ directly into the discussion. The introductory section of verse 13 is vital to Paul's argument at this point; in it he alludes to verse 10 and its base text in order to construct a bridge between "law" and "curse" that is not evident in his base text for verse 13, Deuteronomy 21:23. As in verse 10, so here Paul introduces the base text using the noun form of "curse," while the Septuagint text contains a verb form. Interestingly, Paul seems to transpose the particular verb for "cursed" from Deuteronomy 27:26 onto Deuteronomy 21:23, which, according to the Septuagint, uses a different, though closely related verb, derived from the same root.

The major difference in wording that Paul's citation shows from a Greek translation of Jewish Scriptures is that Deuteronomy 21:23 includes "by God" following "cursed." The two easiest explanations for this variance are that Paul was either working from a different version of the base text that did not include the phrase or Paul left it out. On a related note, Paul leaves out the whole first part of the verse, which explicates the matter at hand in the context of Deuteronomy: the exposure of an already dead (by stoning) body—that is, a corpse—to public viewing. By not including that phrase, Paul's citation fits much more neatly the parallel with Jesus' execution by crucifixion in which, of course, he was hung alive upon the tree, or cross.

An important word and, by extension, concept is introduced almost in passing here given Paul's repetitive use of "curse" language: that is, "redeemed." The word is used fairly broadly in Greek literature for "buying" or "buying out," including purchasing the freedom of a slave. Paul's previous (2:4–5) and upcoming use of the slave metaphor (4:1, 3, 7, 8, 9; and within the Hagar metaphor, 4:24, 25; 5:1) certainly flavors its use here. An interesting and crucial debate within Christian theology arises if one is to ask of 3:13, from whom does Christ make this purchase? Among answers traditionally given are the Devil or God. Paul seems uninterested in answering or clarifying.

Verse 14 closes out this compact set of arguments, and citations with back-to-back statements that grammarians call "purpose clauses"—"in order that"/"so that"—each introduced by the same Greek particle. The first would seem to state baldly, by way of clarification or focus, what Paul has been saying since at least verse 7: in Christ Jesus the blessing of Abraham might come to the Gentiles. So far so good.

Does the second clause simply clarify further—a clarity with a slightly different focus? Perhaps. Just as the first clause brings in "the blessing" (cf. 3:8, 9), Christ Jesus (cf. 3:1, 13), and Abraham (3:6–9) from earlier in Paul's discussion, so the second brings in "faith" (3:6–9, 11, 12) and—reaching back a few more verses—the Spirit (3:2, 3, 5). But, the clause is complicated by two additional components: "we" and "the promise."

The latter is a term that Paul introduces here and uses regularly through the remainder of chapter 3 (16, 17, 18 [twice], 19 [in verb form], 21, 22, 29) and again in 4:21, 22, 29. That said, it is not found in the Abrahamic texts under consideration and is used only one other time by Paul, (2 Cor. 7:1), which appears consistent with its uses here in Galatians. Is Paul, then, using a term of his rivals or, just the opposite, contrasting his "promise" with their "blessing" (a word that is found in the Abrahamic texts)? It may be relevant that the word for "gospel," which is clearly a favorite of Paul's, and "promise" contain the same root word.

As challenging as the question about the usage of "promise" is (their word or Paul's?), all the more does Paul's use of pronouns raise questions throughout this section, perhaps nowhere more so than here. The use of "Gentiles" in 14a is clear and consistent with Paul's understanding and argument as presented. What about the "we"? Does Paul intend Christians broadly—including the Gentiles he has just named; does he mean Jews broadly, Christian and not; or, does he mean particularly Christian Jews? Of those three choices, the first is the easiest and most likely answer. To keep it even simpler, one might take it as reference to himself and the addressees, who are Gentile Christians and so have been named in 14a. By including himself with them via the "we" Paul models and prefigures the negation of difference, which he will get to shortly (3:26–29). More so he indicates that there is no privilege or attainment that he has (for example, via his Jewish identity) that they need or should want (as the rival teachers are, at least in Paul's opinion, indicating through their teaching) in their status as members of the faith community. Verse 14a announces the welcome and opens the door to all, while 14b equalizes the status of all who enter.

In beginning the next phase of the discussion, Paul appeals to his "brothers and sisters" (lit., "siblings"; see comments on 1:2 and 1:11 above), affirming and modeling the (new) family relationship (across lines of difference) that Christians have with each other. He sets up his return to consideration of Abraham in verses 16–18. with a brief discussion "from daily life" regarding "a person's will."

Looming mightily in the background of these verses is the matter of "covenant" and particularly the Abrahamic covenant as described in Genesis 17. Sometimes the challenge for translators is virtually insurmountable. So it it here. The NRSV rightly indicates that Paul is talking about (1) a "will," as in a "last will and testament," in verse 15 and (2) about a biblical, particularly the Abrahamic, "covenant" in verse 17. What is lost in translation is that these two words, "will" and "covenant," translate precisely the same word in Paul's Greek. His addressees would have recognized that immediately. Through the brief and, by design, self-evident statement of verse 15 Paul is beginning to reorient and recast the use of will/covenant away from the rival teachers who doubtless leaned heavily on the covenant language (Gen. 17:2, 4, 7 [twice], 9, 10, 13 [twice], 14) in and around the telling of the circumcision of Abraham in Genesis 17:9–14.

In the discussion of 3:6–9 above, we noticed that Paul uses the same word for "offspring" in Romans as he does here. In Romans 4:16–17, the NRSV translates the word as "descendants," which, indeed, it does standardly mean. The word under consideration is literally "seed," and in the contexts both of the chapters on Abraham in Genesis and Paul's own letter to the Romans, it serves as a collective noun to refer to multiple descendants.

But here, in reference most directly to Genesis 17:10 (though see also 12:7 and 17:9), Paul seizes on the fact that the word is grammatically singular. With that, he forwards his peculiarly christological reading that in entering into covenant with Abraham and his *one* "offspring," God entered into, and "ratified" (v. 17), the Abrahamic covenant through Christ. Paul neatly ignores or passes by the circumcision that marks the Abrahamic covenant (Gen. 17:9–14).

A nuance is lost in the way the NRSV presents the quotes in verse 16 and the shift into verse 17. Within verse 16, as indicated in the NRSV, the verb "say" is used to introduce Paul's point about the singularity, not plurality, of the verb: the biblical text "does not say . . ." However, unlike the NRSV, Paul does not repeat the word "say," but simply uses "but" to introduce what the biblical text "does say." Then, in verse 17, Paul writes, "but I say." That is a telling and, arguably, forthright move on his part and casts his statement as a declaration or a formal teaching (see also Gal. 4:1; interesting parallels—which further stress the "I" by addition of another word—are available in the way Jesus introduces his own teachings vis-à-vis traditional teachings, as found in Matt. 5:22 and parallels).

Paul brings the law back into the discussion, here cast as the newcomer. It is most unlikely that Paul is addressing a problem—the historically or chronologically later-than-Abraham introduction of the Law on Mount Sinai—which had been unconsidered or unaddressed by his fellow Jews including, one presumes, his rival teachers. Though all or most of our evidence comes from rabbinic writings that were codified in the centuries immediately following Paul's, they doubtless reflect earlier responses. For example, *Genesis Rabbah* indicates the sorts of approaches that teachers would take. Rabbi Shimeon is cited as answering the question, "Whence did [Abraham] learn the Torah" or Law, with the answer, "The Holy One . . ." (Neusner, 1985, LXI.I.I). Even more basically, from consideration of Genesis 1:1 on, *Genesis Rabbah* forwards the notion of the preexistence of the law: ". . . the Holy One, blessed be he, consulted the Torah [or, Law] when he created the world" (I.2.F; tr. Jacob Neusner, p. 26 in *Confronting Creation: How Judaism Reads Genesis, an Anthology of Genesis Rabbah*). In sum, the Torah preexists all creation and therefore is available at the time of Abraham, and Abraham didn't need the Law as revealed at Sinai for he knew it directly from God.

Paul will have none of that. Seizing on Exodus 12:40 he points out that the Law postdates God's covenant with Abraham and cannot, and does not, annul it. Then, with a formulation reminiscent of verse 12 ("law . . . faith"), Paul juxtaposes law and promise in verse 18; the two are incompatible. Paul does not use the "covenant" word here, perhaps because direct reference to God granting "to Abraham through" the covenant might immediately recall the circumcision descriptions of Genesis 17. Rather Paul uses "promise."

Paul also introduces in verse 18 the term and concept of "inheritance," which is important within this section and in Galatians more broadly (see "heir" in Gal. 3:29, 4:1, 7, and "inherit" in 4:30 and 5:21). It is, of course, familiar from the Abrahamic narratives in Genesis (e.g., Gen. 15:3, 4; 21:10; 22:17, including a blessing bestowed on Rebekah 24:60). For Paul, the "inheritance" is of a piece with the "promise" (which is summarized in v. 14, picking up on vv. 6–9 [esp. 8–9]) and is considered in some detail in 4:1–7.

LAW AND FAITH
Galatians 3:19–25

3:19 Why then the law? It was added because of transgressions, until the offspring would come to whom the promise had been made; and it was ordained through angels by a mediator. [20] Now a mediator involves more than one party; but God is one.

[21] Is the law then opposed to the promises of God? Certainly not! For if a law had been given that could make alive, then righteousness would indeed come through the law. [22] But the scripture has imprisoned all things under the power of sin, so that what was promised through faith in Jesus Christ might be given to those who believe.

[23] Now before faith came, we were imprisoned and guarded under the law until faith would be revealed. [24] Therefore the law was our disciplinarian until Christ came, so that we might be justified by faith. [25] But now that faith has come, we are no longer subject to a disciplinarian, . . .

Verses 26–29 will pick up directly on the twofold "inheritance" and "promise," but Paul is not finished with the law yet. Of course, what I've just written is a loaded statement, to be sure, and has far broader implications than this letter alone. See, for example, Romans 7 wherein Paul has many things to say about the law, including the plainly complimentary: "So the law is holy, and the commandment is holy and just and good" (Rom. 7:12); "For we know that the law is spiritual" (Rom. 7:14). But that is another time and is to and for people in another place—literally and figuratively. Here Paul has left himself in a bit of a quandary regarding his Galatian addressees. Does he really want them to regard the law as fully other—not "faith," not "promise," not "inheritance," removed from all of God's good dealing with humankind—while the rival teachers are inviting and persuading them more fully into a life within the law? He needs to offer some apology for the law within the system he has constructed and, as he is accustomed to doing throughout this section, he needs to equalize any sense of difference or imbalance.

The question that opens this section is straightforward and comes as an honest response from an imagined interlocutor to Paul's arguments thus far. At the center of the response is a simple construction that the NRSV captures well: "because of transgressions." Now, according to the standard Greek-English Lexicon used in the academic study of New Testament texts (BDAG, 2000, 1079a) the Greek word translated "because of" may either be "indicating the goal" or "indicating the reason." If Paul intends the former, which is likely, then this passage would indicate that the law was added *with the goal of* transgressions.

On the surface that may seem odd. However, it is quite analogous to passages in Romans, such as Romans 5:20, wherein the NRSV "with the result that" is actually better rendered, based on the Greek, "in order that": "law came in order that the trespass might multiply." Romans 4:15 captures such a notion well according to the NRSV: "For the law brings wrath; but where there is no law, neither is there violation"; it is noteworthy that the "violation" of Romans 4:15 and the "transgressions" of Galatians 3:19 translate the same Greek word.

But there is more. The verb Paul chooses is passive, not active—"it was added." Why the passive? Perhaps Paul means to put off consideration of who did the adding until he has finished answering the immediate question. "Because of" or "with the goal of" "transgressions" moves the answer so far, and will be fleshed out a bit more. "Until the offspring would come to whom the promise had been made," moves the answer further and it too will be fleshed out further.

Both of these answers would have found vehement disagreement from contemporary Jewish interlocutors and within contemporary Judaism more broadly. The Torah, for example, was instituted not with the goal of transgressions but, just the opposite, with the goal of curbing them. Such would be an obvious response and it is available, among other places, in the *Letter of Aristeas*, a Greek-language document that includes the story of how the Hebrew Scriptures came to be translated into Greek to form the Septuagint. Therein one learns that the law was given in order that "[we] remain pure in body and soul, free from all vain imaginations" (*Letter of Aristeas*, line 139). As to the delineated time of the Torah—limited to the period from 430 years after Abraham to the coming of Christ—it flies in face of the notion of the eternity of the Torah that we met above in discussion of verse 17; see similarly 2 Esdras 9:37: "the law . . . does not perish but survives in its glory." Indeed, the passive verb—"was added"— illustrates the relatively late and limited role for Torah allowed by Paul.

On the matter of who does the adding, Paul's statements are much more consistent with other familiar, contemporary Jewish descriptions. As we have already seen in the discussion of Paul's use of "angel" in Galatians 1:8, angels were understood to have been present and associated with the giving of the Law at Sinai. Such a description is found, among other places, in the Septuagint version of Deuteronomy 33:2 (see similarly Josephus, *Antiquities*, 15:126). Within the New Testament, Stephen's famous speech contains direct reference to the involvement of angels at Sinai (in the singular, Acts 7:38; in the plural, 7:53). Further, not only are the angels present (so Deut. 33:2, in the Septuagint), and not only is the ordaining (notice, again, a passive verb form here in v. 19) accomplished "through" them (so Acts 7:53), but Paul adds that the angels' agency was accomplished "by" or, literally, "in the hands of" a "mediator." The first phrase indicates Paul's awareness of, and comfort with, phraseology that had become standard in the Septuagint with regard to Moses (see, e.g., Lev. 26:46, Num. 4:37, 41, 45, 49; 9:23; 10:13; 15:23; 17:5; 33:1). Similarly, the term "mediator" simply underscores the importance of Moses' role as God's agent and is consistent with literature contemporary with Paul (Philo, *On the Special Laws*, 1.116).

Paul's presentation of the law thus far appears quite inconsistent with contemporary Jewish understanding of the purpose of the law but quite consistent with contemporary Jewish understandings of the giving of the law. That said, God has yet to be named; though God's name may be indicated by indirect reference to God: the use of the two passive verbs in verse 19 may serve together as a circumlocution to avoid naming God, as is done through the passive verb in verse 16.

When God is introduced into the discussion in verse 21, God is on the side of the law. Though clearly limiting the scope of the law, which is fully consistent with his overarching goal of limiting or cutting off completely the influence of the rival teachers, Paul does not mean to suggest that the law is in any manner opposed to or separate from God or God's promises: "Certainly not!" And though the exclamation point does not exist in the Greek text, one can hear and feel it. Paul uses this distinct phrase, known in Greek rhetoric, at particular points in Galatians (see also 2:17) and several times in Romans.

As with his explanation of the law's purpose in verse 19, so here Paul seems at odds with standard approaches within Judaism. With regard to the discussion of verses 12 and 14 of chapter 1, we saw how Paul uses technical language associated with the Pharisaic or Rabbinic traditions of the day, codified in a well-known work, the *Pirke Avot*, or *Fathers of Rabbi Nathan*.

Within that text the famous Rabbi Hillel is credited with this statement: ". . . the more Law [or, *Torah*], the more life . . ." (2.8). It is hard to believe that Paul, trained as he is in Pharisaism, is not familiar with that or similar sayings. Similarly, it is likely that the rival teachers, promoting, as they do, acceptance of the law by these new Gentiles Christians, are familiar with and even promote such an understanding of law. Paul will have none of it.

Indirectly returning to the compact set of statements and proof texts in 3:10–14 and to his broader discussion of faith, Paul reminds his listeners that it is faith, not law, that equates to life. They have become Christians through the receiving of the Spirit (3:2), and that has and will continue to mark their "experience" (3:4) as Christians. What is more, just as "scripture" is the actor in 3:8 who foresaw God's action in welcoming and justifying "the Gentiles by faith" and so worked in and through Abraham to accomplish that, so in verse 22 it is "scripture" that "imprisoned all things under the power of sin."

Through what mechanism does Scripture accomplish this? Through the law. On some level this puts Abraham and the law in parallel positions—both being agents or mechanisms employed by "scripture" in service of God's eventual revealing of "faith." The word for "reveal" used here is the technical term for "revelation," as in the "book of the Revelation" that we know and consistent with language Paul has already used in chapter 1 (see vv. 1:12, 15–16; cf. 1:4) suggesting that Paul is drawing on, and rooting his teaching in, Jewish understandings and expectations of the end times.

On another level, Scripture's action through the law is subordinated to Scripture's action through Abraham because the promise to Abraham came first, sets the stage for the law, and holds pride of place for God's action on behalf of "the Gentiles." Consistent with his focus throughout the letter, from verse 8 Paul has concerned himself with God's promise regarding "the Gentiles." And that is Paul's concern here: God's action on behalf of Gentiles through Christ. He is not arguing for or against any position regarding Judaism *as* Judaism. Consistent with his agenda throughout this letter he is mounting an argument about how to welcome Gentile Christians into the full community and full benefit of being God's people. His argument is against rival teachers who are promoting the notion that Gentile Christians practice Jewish law.

But then who is the "we" in verses 23–24? He must be talking about Jews and Judaism, no?

That would seem an obvious and comfortable (on some level) answer, and it may be *the* answer. However, important details and movements within the letter indicate otherwise and would, at the very least, introduce a level of ambiguity or openness: (1) As we have already seen in verses 13–14, there are difficulties in taking the "we" to refer to one or another hard and fast category or collective—Jews, Jewish Christians, all Christians (Jew and Gentile), etc.—whereas taken on its simplest level, referring to Paul and his (Gentile Christian) addressees, the "we" works. (2) Paul has been seeking to erase the distinction between Jew and Gentile (see 2:15–16, 26–29) and other regularly distinguished groups or collectives; so reinforcing such distinction via a we/you pronominal divide would at this point seem contradictory to the thrust of his arguments. (Paul will continue to use "you" to refer to his addressees, while his "we" is inclusive of "you" Galatians and himself). (3) Paul clearly states in verse 22 that Scripture has "imprisoned *all things*," its action not being limited to a Jewish sphere. And (4) in chapter 4 Paul seems to be at pains to recall and equate *both* the Gentile experience and Jewish experience of being enslaved (4:8) under law (4:3–5) to the point of collecting all of that experience via a category "elemental spirits," which includes natural elements worshiped as divinities among the pagans. Clearly Paul is questioning categories that others (then and now) may consider hard and fast and doing so with a purpose (as becomes increasingly clear in the next section)!

The image of the "disciplinarian," or pedagogue, would be familiar to anyone in and around Hellenistic cities of any size. Such a character, normally a slave, would attend schoolboys to and from their lessons. His role was both guardian and disciplinarian. Upon reaching a mature age, the youth would become free of his pedagogue. Having put the metaphor in place, Paul does not draw any analogy between the "we" and the one in care of the "disciplinarian." No advance or attainment on the part of the "we" prompts the severing of ties with the disciplinarian, the law. Simply, "faith has come" (which sends the reader back to Paul's discussions of faith in 2:16; 3:10; and throughout) so "we are no longer subject to a disciplinarian."

FAITH, BAPTISM, AND INHERITANCE
Galatians 3:26–29

> 3:26 . . . for in Christ Jesus you are all children of God through faith. [27] As many of you as were baptized into Christ have clothed yourselves with Christ. [28] There is no longer Jew or Greek, there is no longer slave or free, there is no longer male and female; for all of you are one in Christ Jesus. [29] And if you belong to Christ, then you are Abraham's offspring, heirs according to the promise.

For many familiar with Paul, including those who find themselves uncomfortable or at odds with some or much of what Paul writes, this is a favorite passage. There are good reasons for that, tied into one's worldview: self-identity; relationship with God, Christ, and church. How does it forward Paul's concerns, and how might it have resonated with Paul's addressees in Galatians?

In Greek, the first word that appears in verse 26 is "all," an indication of the direction he will take his addressees in these few verses. It also may suggest that he is countering a position of the rival teachers or activity on the part of some of the Galatians. Are the teachers teaching or suggesting that *not* all of the Galatians, as recently baptized Gentile Christians, are "children of God"?

Relevant here is Paul's use of "children of Abraham" in 3:7 as discussed above. In this verse as in 3:7, the particular phrase used is not found elsewhere in Paul's letters as we have them (cf. Gal. 4:6–7 and 2 Cor. 6:18 for similar phrases). Meanwhile, it is a recurring one in the Hebrew Bible and is found in contemporary Jewish literature regarding the status of the Jewish people. And within the Jewish literature of the time, it is the *Psalms of Solomon* 17.27 that may be the most relevant to Paul and to this passage, because it describes the coming messiah, includes the word "all" in connection with "sons," and was likely written by a first-century Pharisaic author.

The phrase, "children of God," is further defined by Paul. The placement of "in Christ Jesus" is curious in the NRSV translation. Based on its placement in the Greek text, it is most easily and readily read as following "through faith"; in other words, through faith in Jesus Christ. Unlike other similar phrases in the letter (see Gal. 2:16) this one is unambiguous regarding faith *in* Jesus Christ. In the earliest extant manuscript of this text it simply reads "through Christ Jesus."

As for the ongoing matter of pronouns through this section, it is striking here that after having established the "we" in verses 13–14, and using it through verse 25, Paul switches abruptly to the second person plural form of address: "you" Galatians. "We" would have worked just fine, offhand. Why the switch?

First, for reasons that will be considered more below, it appears that in verses 26–28 Paul is quoting directly from a baptismal formula or liturgy. That very formula may well have used "you," as the one leading the liturgy addresses those about to be baptized. Further, this first line is likely drawn directly from biblical literature, perhaps Deuteronomy 14:1, which reads "you are children of the LORD your God." Further, Paul is countering the rivals' teachings here and wants to put the focus squarely on the Galatian addressees who have been baptized and have become full members of the community. In other words, he is talking to "you" and he wants "you" to listen.

A simple and exciting possibility here is that in verses 26–28 Paul is reminding and redirecting the Galatians through words familiar from teaching they received from Paul about baptism and their own experience of baptism, perhaps even including words and phrases that served as part of their baptismal ceremony. There are several indicators: (1) The first (v. 26) and last (v. 28d) phrases are parallel; (2) the dense, repetitive form of the middle phrases (v. 28a, b, c) is indicative of the language of formula; (3) the second line names baptism. Further, in the context of this letter, there is no need for Paul to state verses 28b and c; that is, within Galatians he has no stated agenda regarding "slave or free" or "male and female" either leading up to or following these verses. Maybe they are simply part of the baptismal liturgy that Paul is quoting and that the Galatians experienced.

Though there are no other places in Paul's letters where he seems to quote so directly from a liturgy, there are parallels that support the possibility that this may be indeed be a baptismal liturgy. The closest, is 1 Corinthians 12:13: "For in one Spirit we were all baptized into one body—Jews or Greeks, slaves or free—and we were all made to drink of one Spirit." It varies from Galatians 3:26–28 by using the first person plural, "we," and, while including close parallels to the first and second formulaic phrase in Galatians 3:28, it does not contain a parallel to the third. Colossians 3:9–11 is often cited as well; it contains the same two—Jew, Greek; slave, free—as does 1 Corinthians 12:13, though in expanded form, and also includes the clothing metaphor found in Galatians 3:27. Whether Paul created the very liturgy he seems to be quoting from in Galatians 3:26–28, borrowed it wholesale, or modified a liturgy he had learned earlier on is another, likely unanswerable, question. A related question, raised by this brief consideration of parallels, is whether—and to what degree—the baptismal liturgies themselves varied among the Pauline churches. Of course, the manner and (varying) degree to which Paul himself engaged in baptizing is another related question (see 1 Cor. 1:14–17).

Though verse 27 contains the sole direct mention of baptism in the letter, the whole of this section most likely re-creates, in some instances word for word, parts of an ancient Christian baptismal liturgy. Early baptismal pools derived from the Jewish ritual bath called a *mikveh*. In Paul's time, these small, recessed stone pools typically had staircases (usually of three or four steps) on either side that descended into the water. Paul imagines a baptismal candidate standing at one side of the pool. He or she disrobes, steps down into the pool, is baptized, and then steps out of the pool to be robed by an attendant on the opposite side. All those preparing for baptism—whether male or female, slave or free, Jew or Greek—are robed with identical robes after they emerge from the pool (for helpful descriptions, with citations of primary literature, see Meeks, *The First Urban Christians*, esp. 87–88, 150–52).

The metaphor of being clothed is familiar in a number of passages within the Pauline letters, which all appear, in varying ways, to draw on and allude to baptismal practice. We have already referenced Colossians 3:9–10, which reads, ". . . seeing that you have stripped off the old self with its practices and have clothed yourselves with the new self, which is being renewed in knowledge according to the image of its creator." The new garment is not Christ but "the new self," "renewed" "according to the image of its creator" and, as one reads on, informed by "Christ" (Col. 3:11; cf. Gal. 6:15). Ephesians 4:24 includes the command to "clothe yourselves with the new self, created according to the likeness of God. . . ." Romans 13:12, Ephesians 6:11, and 1 Thessalonians 5:18 employ the clothing metaphor with regard to military armaments, and equipping oneself for new life and new identity in Christ. Romans 13:14 and 1 Corinthians 15:53–54 are also relevant. One can imagine that "clothing yourself with Christ" and similar language was part of Paul's teaching in founding Christian communities and preparing individuals and groups for baptism.

Was something akin to Romans 6:3–4 also part of Paul's teaching around baptism at this time? There he writes: "Do you not know that all of us who have been baptized into Christ Jesus were baptized into his death? Therefore we have been buried with him by baptism into death, so that . . . we too might walk in newness of life." It is interesting that the ingredients for such appear to be present in Galatians (see 2:19–20). However, Paul does not use such language here.

From the "clothing" metaphor Paul moves his addressees into the dense statements of verse 28. These are noteworthy for their dramatic presentation of three pairs of opposites, the first being the one immediately relevant to Paul's argument within the text. We have seen that Paul has made several moves in the direction of erasing distinctions. So here the opposites are named and grouped together only to be followed by the statement "for all of you are one. . . ."

The baldness and simplicity of that final statement within the verse is notable. What does it mean? What can it possibly mean? Clearly, the first statement flies in the face of the rivals' approach to the matter of how to bring Gentiles further into the people of God. By their teaching that Gentile Christians should follow and practice (all or some significant portion of) the Jewish laws, they are maintaining and reinforcing the binary division of the world that is familiar and taken for granted among contemporary Jews (see discussion of 2:15 above).

What of the second and third items, or of the full package of the three sets of two? In his commentary on Galatians, J. Louis Martyn considers an overarching, apocalyptic theme within his baptismal formula and in Paul's presentation in chapters 3 and 4 more broadly: "To pronounce the nonexistence of these opposites is to announce nothing less than the end of the cosmos" (p. 376). In the popular speech of our day, we might say that the presentation of the dissolution of these opposites through their oneness "in Christ" may be announcing "the end of the world as we know it." And frankly, that is what Paul is after vis-à-vis his rivals—specifically, the end of the Jew-Gentile division within the Christian community. Further, Martyn's work serves to reinforce the idea that there are apocalyptic undertones to the clothing language in the previous verse; it is about outfitting the newly faithful for a new reality. There are other inklings of apocalyptic or end-of-time thinking within these pairs. A quick glance at Mark 12:25 suggests just such a context for the third pair: "For when they rise from the dead, they neither marry nor are given in marriage. . . ."

Returning to Paul, one might understand several of the teachings in 1 Corinthians 7 as practical and moral teachings in light of this baptismal formula and its apocalyptic context. For example, regarding the male-female pair, 1 Corinthians 7:29: "I mean, brothers and sisters, the appointed time has grown short; from now on, let even those who have wives be as though they had none. . . ." Similarly 1 Corinthians 7:18 on the subject of the Jew-Greek pair: "Was anyone at the time of his call already circumcised? Let him not seek to remove the marks of circumcision. Was anyone at the time of his call uncircumcised? Let him not seek circumcision." And what of the remaining pair from Galatians 3:28? See 1 Corinthians 7:21–22: "Were you a slave when called? Do not be concerned about it. Even if you can gain your freedom, make use of your present condition now more than ever. For whoever was called in the Lord as a slave is a freed person belonging to the Lord, just as whoever was free when called is a slave of Christ."

What is the point? That the quotes from 1 Corinthians are immediately relevant either to the context in Galatians or to ours today? Not at all. Rather, that just as Paul's Corinthian teachings suggest particular application of such a baptismal formula as is found in Galatians, so too do they suggest what the simple statements that "there is no longer" any distinction within these pairings of oppositions and that "all of you are one in Christ Jesus" might mean, at least for Paul. For Paul, verse 28 neither pronounces nor suggests the erasure of difference per se. More simply, and on some level more profoundly, it announces that "in Christ" those differences count for nothing (see discussion of 4:7, below).

Verse 29 is a key verse in this broad section. It not only summarizes and punctuates much of what Paul has written about in chapter 3, it also moves his argument forward. Set up as simple conditional sentence—if x, then y—the condition is actually a ruse since we know that "you" all do belong and therefore are "Abraham's offspring" and therefore are "heirs according to the promise." The radicalness of the pronouncement plays on at least two levels.

First, that each of the members of the three pairs could be considered an "heir" is, simply on the face of it, radical. The entire letter, as we have seen, is about the challenge and complication of bringing Gentiles into the community of Christ, with the rivals suggesting or demanding that there needs to be (at least some) acceptance of Jewish practice for Gentiles. In keeping with the societal structures of the time, for either a slave or a female to be pronounced "heir," especially when there are free persons and males within the same household, would be unusual at least, more likely unheard of. But, here it is.

Secondly there is the matter of the "offspring," or seed. Just sentences earlier, Paul based an entire plank of his argument on the idea that "offspring" refers to "one person, who is Christ." Here, he pronounces that the plurality of his addressees, in other words "you" (plural) are "Abraham's offspring"! Has Paul forgotten his own argument regarding the singularity of the offspring? No. He is forwarding a very inclusive and relational ecclesiology. The relationship between "you" (plural) and

"Christ" within the protasis—the "if" part—of verse 29 is even simpler than stated in the NRSV: "if you are of Christ." For Paul, being "of Christ" is to take on or embody Christ's role as "offspring." Of course the "you" who does that embodying is made up of a plurality of differently defined and distinguished groups, some of whom enjoy a relatively high level of status and access to resources and opportunity in the "real" world and some of whom do not. No matter. The plurality stands in Christ's stead and takes on Christ's role as "offspring"; *all* who "are one in Christ Jesus" are "heirs."

SLAVERY, FREEDOM, ADOPTION, AND INHERITANCE
Galatians 4:1–7

> 4:1 My point is this: heirs, as long as they are minors, are no better than slaves, though they are the owners of all the property; [2] but they remain under guardians and trustees until the date set by the father. [3] So with us; while we were minors, we were enslaved to the elemental spirits of the world. [4] But when the fullness of time had come, God sent his Son, born of a woman, born under the law, [5] in order to redeem those who were under the law, so that we might receive adoption as children. [6] And because you are children, God has sent the Spirit of his Son into our hearts, crying, Abba! Father! [7] So you are no longer a slave but a child, and if a child then also an heir, through God.

Within these verses, Paul teases out that which he has stated in the previous section, concerning the baptismal formula. Of the three pairings of opposites, the one most clearly present here is that of "slave . . . free." That said, the other two are also very much in play, as we will see.

Paul introduces the discussion within these verses with the same construction he uses in 3:17 (see discussion above) and so marks what follows particularly as a teaching or declaration. He then begins to develop that teaching by way of an extended metaphor, picking up directly on the slave-free pairing within 3:28. In keeping with broad and particular norms and legal codes of the day, the "heir" is presumed free, as opposed to being a slave.

Paul is painting with a broad rhetorical brush in order to equalize the members of the "slave . . . free" pairing. Are the presumed legal heirs really "no better than slaves"? Regarding status, Roman legal code would indicate otherwise, but Paul's rhetorical point is made. Are they under "guardians and trustees"? Well, *yes* to the first (which is a technical term paralleled, by "legal guardian" in our discourse and practice) and *not quite* to the second. Paul might have chosen more proper, technical language for the second term; the NRSV seems to presume such, since the broader term Paul uses might better be reflected with the English, "administrator." But again, Paul has made his rhetorical point.

Regarding the male-female pairing of opposites in 3:28, women did enjoy some, if limited, rights of inheritance under Roman law at the time of Paul's writing (and had since the days of the Republic). The way Paul introduces the subject here presumes a male, as opposed to female, heir. How would his addressees have known that? Because of the statement in 4:2, "until the date set by the father." According to Roman law, a female heir remains under the power of her father until his death. At that point, what inheritance there might be would transfer to her, to be controlled by her husband—that is, presuming she is married. And on that score, under Augustus Caesar and imperial Rome, incentives were added through the Julian Laws to assure a high rate of marriage: women of marrying age who would not marry were barred from receiving inheritances. Setting up the extended metaphor as a male heir is in keeping with the contrasting of opposites in 3:28 and 4:1.

What of the opposing pair, Jew-Greek? Like the male-female pairing, it is not overtly named, but is very much present. First, recall that Paul initially introduced the notion of "inheritance" in 3:18 in conjunction with a discussion regarding Abraham. "Inheritance" is a term familiar within the Abrahamic narratives in Genesis, and may well be a term and concept used by the rival teachers to forward their position that Gentiles coming into the Christian fold do not have full status as heirs of Abraham. The use of the term "inheritance" in the context of this letter and the broader context within which it sits serves to recall the Jew-Greek pairing.

Paul ups the ante a bit in verse 3. Paul's use of pronouns is notoriously difficult to follow throughout this section of the letter. The best presumption may be the simplest: "we" = Paul (the letter writer) and the Galatians (the letter's addressees). Other options clearly exist and to some degree work on different levels. It is perhaps in 4:3–5 that Paul's play with the pronouns is most nimble and creative.

If the "we" here equates solely to Jews or—more in keeping with the context of the letter—Jewish Christians, then notice how outrageous and, on some level, ridiculous is the content of verse 3: *Jews* "enslaved to the elemental spirits"? That makes no sense. Such would be akin to stating within a discussion of American political history that during the period of the cold war American citizens were governed under a system of Communism. As noted in the discussion of 3:23–24 above, these "elemental spirits," in Jewish discourse, refer to natural elements worshiped as divinities among the pagans (see also discussion below on 4:8). In that sense, the Jewish law could not stand as more of a contrast, providing, as it does, a sense of identity and relationship with (the one, Jewish) God.

Of course, if one takes the "we" to include the simple binary pair of writer (Paul) and addressees (Galatians), the statement might be even more outrageous. Paul, a Jew and a Christian, is equating the Jewish experience with which he identifies with the Galatians' Gentile experience. Further, he is placing the whole of it under "the elemental spirits" thereby forwarding outrageous proposals on two matters: (1) that one already considered, which equates Jewish law with pagan "elemental spirits" and (2) suggesting that the two separate and separable experiences, Jewish and Gentile, are equivalent.

Read in light of this simple sense of "we," verse 5 would then simply flip the equation. Whereas "we" (representing both Jew and Gentile) were under "elemental spirits" in verse 3, it is "those who were under the law" who now appear to equate with the "we." So, strange as it seems, Gentiles are being posited to have joined with Jews for a period of time under the law. By way of circling back to the first proposed reading of "we" above, if one presumes a Jewish or Jewish-Christian "we," then verse 6 marks the point of full inclusion and verse 3 stands as an outrageous equation of law with "elemental spirits." At the very least Paul has proven himself a nimble rhetorician who is at pains to draw together the experiences of his own identity group (Jews) with that of the Galatians (Gentiles) to whom he is writing.

There are several elements within the dense language of 4:4–6 that suggest Paul is quoting or alluding to Christian and more broadly Jewish formulaic expressions. Interestingly, the first phrase is both familiar and oddly unfamiliar. "The fullness of time" would appear to pick up on Jewish or Christian discussion of the end times (see, Mark 1:15; Eph. 1:10). However, Paul does not use the familiar word for "time" or season found in those texts and more broadly in apocalyptic contexts (Mark 13:33; Rev. 1:3; 22:10; within Paul; Rom. 13:11; 1 Thess. 5:1). Rather, he uses a word referring more to chronological time, a word that is employed in contracts. Is this another example of Paul being a nimble rhetorician, calling up apocalyptic speculation, and perhaps phraseology familiar (already) among Christians to describe God's action in Christ on the one hand, while on the other reinforcing the notion that the time of the law was for a set—as if contracted—period of time (see 3:17, 19)?

The next phrase picks up on a motif familiar within this early period of Christianity. Or does it? The (likely) earliest Christian description we have of this event renders it via Christ's own action of "emptying" himself (see the Christ Hymn of Phil. 2:5). Paul uses this verb only here and in verse 6, with the latter describing the Holy Spirit, not the Son. What does seem clear is that Paul is picking up on broader Jewish descriptions, both contemporary and within biblical tradition, of God sending out beings from heaven (of Wisdom, see Wisdom of Solomon 9:10; of an angel, Gen. 24:40; of the spirit, Psalm 104:30 [esp. in the Septuagint version, wherein it is numbered 103:30]). That broader Jewish context accounts for the use of the verb both here and in verse 6.

The phrase "born of woman" sounds, offhand, creedal to Christian ears, and indeed may be so, though evidence in this early period is scant. The least that can be said is that the phraseology here is consistent with later creedal statements. Reference to the Christ Hymn of Philippians 2:5–11 shows this phrase: "being born in human likeness." Likely that is what the phrase here in Galatians 4:5 is intended to communicate and how it would have been heard.

The word for "redeem" is used within Paul's letters only in Galatians; here and in 3:13 (see discussion above). In both cases the redeeming is accomplished vis-à-vis the law, though here with the broader description of "elemental spirits" (v. 3) looming behind the expanded sense of law to include both Jewish and Gentile experience. The slavery metaphor developed in verses 1–3 informs verse 5. Though, as indicated in the discussion regarding 3:13, "redeem" is used in varying contexts within the New Testament and in other Greek literature. It can be, and was, employed in a technical sense with regard to slavery to indicate manumission: that is, the purchasing of a slave's freedom. Also noted above about the debate that becomes crucial within Christian theology from the earliest centuries through today, Paul does not indicate from whom it is that Christ makes this purchase on behalf of those "enslaved."

Things are "lost in translation." With regard to language and concepts regarding "son" and sonship language, that is certainly the case in these verses. The NRSV translation is perfectly reasonable and conveys well the meaning of Paul's words: "that we might receive adoption as children." The English "adoption as children" translates one compound Greek verb used to indicate adoption. And "children" captures fairly that part of the compound word that indicates male child in the singular yet in the plural is used as the universal to indicate a plurality of children, both male and female. Consistent with that, the familiar, biblical phrase "sons of Israel," or "sons of God," is often rightly translated "children of Israel" or "children of God" as the word is therein being used as the universal plural.

What is lost in the perfectly reasonable translation, "children," in verse 5 is the juxtaposition of God's "Son" in verse 4 with "adoption as *sons*" (i.e., children, emphasis mine) in verse 5. That is, the consistent use of the same word, Son/sons (perhaps one could translate the pair as Child/children) is used to indicate God's one son, Christ, and God's whole people. Such a pattern is consistent with the striking juxtaposition noted above about the use of "offspring" in 3:16 to refer to Christ and in 3:29 to refer to "you" all, the plurality of God's people.

A similar argument applies to the tightly packed language of verses 6–7. Here the same Greek word is simply repeated three times for "Son . . . child . . . child." Paul's Galatian addressees would have heard the same word and would have naturally equated each use with the others.

Further, notice that each usage is in the singular. This word in the singular unambiguously means male child. What if one steps back and takes that seriously? What results? First, each child, each "*son*" (if you will), is labeled with precisely the same label as Christ, God's one "Son" who "redeemed" us. This is consistent with God's infusion of "the Spirit of [God's] Son into our hearts" and with equating Christ and God's people in verses 4–5 and in 3:16, 29 as just discussed. But there is more. In light of the pairings of opposites from 3:28, what results? (1) Vis-à-vis Jew-Greek, all—not just the Jew—are held with the biblical designation God's son (see, e.g., Exod. 4:22). (2) Vis-à-vis slave-free, all are designated free and not only free, but all are "son" within God's household. (3) Vis-à-vis male-female, all are designated via the male label "son." In light of the legal codes of the day, not to mention a host of unwritten norms, women were discriminated against in many ways even though they did enjoy some, limited rights to inheritance. Here, as "son," women, slaves, and Gentiles are fully "heir" to God's household. Unheard of! Yes, that is the point. And there is no "an" in Paul's language; simply, and profoundly, all are "heir."

In 4:7 Paul is not countering the dominant, presumed societal paradigms at all. Quite the opposite, he assumes them at this juncture in order to make a point about the community of faith. "Son" and "heir" are the presumed positions of status and are simply proposed as such. The radicalness of this verse is in positing for those considered other or outsider the same level of status afforded the inside, presumptive heir. Taken together, 3:28 and 4:7 stand as a kind of tour de force, with 3:28 positing dissolution of difference and 4:7 positing full and same recognition and benefit for all in God's household. Each verse chips away at the rivals' teachings in different ways.

11. Remember When. Now.
Galatians 4:8–20

In the brief introduction to the comments on 3:6–4:7 it is noted that there are distinct similarities between 3:1–5 and 4:8–20. In both sections, Paul calls the Galatians to remember the past. Both their past with him and their further past, prior to their conversion, are directly referenced.

(RE)ENSLAVED
Galatians 4:8–11

> 4:8 **Formerly, when you did not know God, you were enslaved to the beings that by nature are not gods.** [9] **Now, however, that you have come to know God, or rather to be known by God, how can you turn back again to the weak and beggarly elemental spirits? How can you want to be enslaved to them again?** [10] **You are observing special days, and months, and seasons, and years.** [11] **I am afraid that my work for you may have been wasted.**

As neatly as these verses work together with those of 3:1–5 (see comments preceding 3:6 above) they also play off of, and build on, 4:1–7. A strong and simple contrastive "but" in the Greek is captured by "Formerly" in the NRSV. Having neatly and forcefully stated his addressees' status as full heirs within God's household, Paul now brings them back to the time of their enslavement (4:1). For the Gentile Galatians that time, of course, is the time before their conversion. Assuming a position that is perfectly consistent with common Jewish perception of Gentile religious understanding and practice (which was doubtless shared also by the rival teachers), Paul reminds the Galatians that prior to their conversion, when they "did not know God," they were "enslaved to beings that by nature are not gods." The sentiment is consistent with that mentioned in discussions of both 4:3 and 3:23–24 above and is captured well in Wisdom of Solomon 13:1–2:

For all people who were ignorant of God were foolish by nature;
and they were unable from the good things that are seen to know
   the one who exists,
nor did they recognize the artisan while paying heed to his works,
but they supposed that either fire or wind or swift air,
or the circle of the stars, or turbulent water,
or the luminaries of heaven were the gods that rule the world.

One can imagine that Paul's own teaching and the teaching of the rival teachers might have contained some of these very elements. Within Paul's letters, Romans 1:23 and 25 show direct similarities with the quotation above.

In Paul's earliest extant letter, 1 Thessalonians, in which he similarly recalls his Gentile addressees' pagan past (1 Thess. 1:9), he employs the same verb that is translated here "enslaved." Therein he uses it in the active voice and in a positive manner: the Thessalonians, Paul writes, "turn" from their pagan ways "to serve" or "to be slaves to . . . [God]" (1 Thess. 1:9). In Galatians 4:8–9, however, the imagery of slavery is decidedly negative and parallel to its usage in 4:3. Following the clear and dramatic pronounce-ment of sonship and inheritance in 4:1–7, it clearly denotes a backsliding—what amounts to a *re*-enslavement. As such, within the immediate context and the broader context of the whole letter, it also serves to redefine the rival teachers and their Law-centered position as akin to backsliding.

In another circumstance, one can imagine a rival teacher speaking verse 9 virtually word for word. That circumstance would be the actual return of a Gentile individual or group of Gentiles to pagan practices. Here, of course, Paul's concern is quite different. He is countering these recent Gentile converts' forays into adopting Jewish practices under the influ-ence of the rival teachers.

Paul has already set a pattern of bringing together terms, concepts, and categories that one would not expect (see 3:23–24, 3:28, and 4:1–7, esp. 4:3); so here. There is great irony in this equation of Jewish law with pagan observance of "elemental spirits." Though the rival teachers would have disagreed vehemently, the rhetorical gain for Paul is significant. By equating what would doubtless have been understood and welcomed as a maturing in faith by the rival teachers (the adoption of Jewish practices by these Gentile converts) with backsliding, Paul means to stake out his posi-tion as the position of integrity (cf. Gal. 1:6–7).

The language in the first part of verse 9 is built around the particular word for "know" from which the term "gnostic" derives and with which Gnosticism was associated in the ancient world and now. Does Paul's usage here suggest gnostic tendencies or context (that is, a kind of intimate or "inside" knowledge premised on philosophical or mystical speculation which posits a God[head] beyond the generally recognized creator God and "known" only by some)? Likely not. Paul is drawing directly on (Greek language) biblical tradition. In the Septuagint version of Psalm 79:6 (78:6 in the Septuagint) regarding "the nations [or "Gentiles"] that do not know" God, the verb used is the same one that Paul uses here. Of course, relative to that Psalm passage, Paul has made the negative a positive: these Gentiles do "know" God.

No sooner has Paul stated that the Galatians have come to know God then he rhetorically corrects himself: it is not a matter of knowing God but rather "to be known by" God. Here, too, Paul is drawing directly on biblical tradition. In Psalm 139:1–2 (138:1–2 in the Septuagint), for example, the psalmist declares to God: "You have searched me and known me. You know when I sit down and when I rise up." Among Paul's letters, it is within the Corinthian correspondences that he pursues this matter in more depth, perhaps no more so than in 1 Corinthians 8:1–3: ". . . Knowledge puffs up, love builds up. Anyone who claims to know something does not yet have the necessary knowledge; but anyone who loves God is known by him" (cf. 1 Cor. 13:12; 2 Cor. 4:6). Clearly in the Corinthian passage, it is not human knowledge of God that equates to being known by God; indeed, knowledge of a type that is measurable or claimable in human terms will never be sufficient or necessary. Consistently in both 1 Corinthians (12:4, 7) and Galatians (3:4), it is the presence of God's Spirit that effects the "manifestation" (1 Corinthians) or "experience" (Galatians) of God.

So, to go back to the initial question put to this verse regarding "knowledge" and its possible gnostic context or tendencies, Paul here is countering any form of claimed religious experience that bases itself in human understanding or achievement. Here he calls the Galatians back to God's action on their behalf (cf. Gal. 3:1–5).

Verse 10 serves on some level as a kind of eye of the storm. Swirling all around it is Paul's multilayered and creative (re)statement of his "gospel" and countering of the rival teachers' position. Here is a simple charge or, if you will, an itemized list of four connected charges, which on the surface reads quite simply. What is going on?

Paul is fusing together two opposites (see Gal. 3:28) as he has been doing consistently in 4:3 and in the preceding verse. On the surface, and in light of a simple, unironic reading of verse 9, he is referring to pagan observance. We have already seen in the citation from Wisdom of Solomon 13:1–2, above, a statement of typical Jewish polemic against pagan equating of the "circle of the stars" and the "luminaries of heavens" with divinities (see Wisdom of Solomon 13:18 for the use of "weak," as in v. 9 herein). In actuality Paul is referring (and responding) not to the Galatians' backsliding but to their desire to take on Jewish practices, such as circumcision and (here) observance of Sabbath and holidays. On that score, in *Antiquities*, Josephus uses precisely the same word for "observing" in reference to the keeping of the Sabbath (14.264; cf. 3.91, 11.294).

Paul feigns, or perhaps simply and honestly states, that he is "afraid" in verse 11. The object of his fear is "you," a simple point of grammar in the Greek text that is lost in the English of the NRSV. Paul is "afraid with regard to you." What he fears more specifically, as indicated in the NRSV, is that his "work for you may have been wasted." These are harsh words, tempered somewhat by the quick retort he has already offered to his own statement in 3:4: the posited "nothing" in 3:4 and the "wasted" in this verse translate the same Greek adjective. Here, as there, one can almost hear Paul echoing for himself, "if it really was wasted." And with that he moves to direct appeal.

(RE)FORMED
Galatians 4:12–20

> 4:12 Friends, I beg you, become as I am, for I also have become as you are. You have done me no wrong. [13] You know that it was because of a physical infirmity that I first announced the gospel to you; [14] though my condition put you to the test, you did not scorn or despise me, but welcomed me as an angel of God, as Christ Jesus. [15] What has become of that goodwill you felt? For I testify that, had it been possible, you would have torn out your eyes and given them to me. [16] Have I now become your enemy by telling you the truth? [17] They make much of you, but for no good purpose; they want to exclude you, so that you may make much of them. [18] It is good to be made much of for a good purpose at all times, and not only when I am present with you. [19] My little children, for whom I am again in the pain of childbirth until Christ is formed in you, [20] I wish I were present with you now and could change my tone, for I am perplexed about you.

This very important section begins with a direct appeal. The NRSV translation, "Friends," is unfortunately misleading. Paul appeals to his addressees not as his friends, but as his family members or "Siblings." Here the alternative translation, "Brothers," (or "Brothers and Sisters") is preferable. As discussed in the comments on 1:2 regarding the phrase translated "members of God's family" (and alternatively, "all the brothers") in the NRSV, the plural of the Greek word for "brother" serves as the universal to refer to a collective of two or more siblings of both genders. Family imagery occurs in the arguments and descriptions of chapter 3 (v. 26) and 4 (v. 1–7). In these verses, Paul seizes on such kinship language in order to describe himself and his addressees together and separately (see v. 19 wherein they are "children" and he, interestingly, is in the role of mother).

From his earliest letter, Paul uses "siblings" as a form of address for those in the community (see 1 Thess. 1:4; 2:1,7, 9, 14, 17; 4:1, 9; 5:12). In so doing, he can both affirm and undercut an established paradigm for expressing the teacher-student relationship. In Philippians 3:17, for example, he sets himself up as the paradigm for the community to imitate: "Brothers and sisters, join in imitating me. . . ." Here, there is no such overt imitation language. Indeed, the language is completely reciprocal. It is he, the one in the role of teacher or "apostle" (Gal. 1:1), who proffers the command to be or "become." The relationship of the first *as* phrase— "become *as* I am"—to the second *as* phrase—"I also have become *as* you are" (emphasis mine)—is more compact and more parallel in Greek: "become as I, for even I as you. . . ." The NRSV translation captures what is a likely implication within Paul's command: that he (a Jew) *has become* like them (Gentiles) in not observing points of Jewish law any longer (cf. 2:11–21). Further, though the NRSV alternative translation, "Brothers" (and even better, "brothers and sisters" or "siblings"), is very much to be preferred for reasons discussed above, the NRSV's "Friends" does capture something important within this passage, which has further repercussions throughout Paul's appeal. Via the paralleling of the "I . . . you," Paul is not only introducing some play into the teacher-student paradigm, but is also appealing to the paradigm of friendship. For example, Cicero, who for a time made his office as provincial governor in Tarsus (Paul's home town, according to Acts) writes: "The one who looks on a true friend looks as if on a kind of model for oneself" (*On Friendship*, 23). Prior to that, Cicero identifies "mutual benefit" or reciprocity as a mark of true friendship (*On Friendship*, 22). Paul's appeal to the Galatians is consistent with Cicero's understanding of friendship, as Paul continues.

The language of verse 13 is simple: it is "because of" or "on account of" some unexplained "physical infirmity" that Paul initially "announced the gospel" to the Galatians. Clearly, it was not part of his broad or specific planning to stay in Galatia long enough to introduce his gospel and found churches here. But circumstances dictated otherwise. What the illness or weakness may have been is not possible to know with any certainty. An immediate clue may lie in verse 15. Was Paul suffering from some condition involving temporary blindness? Further, is there any relationship between this condition and the equally vague "thorn . . . in the flesh" that he describes in 2 Corinthians 12:7? There are deeper parallels between these two passages than is immediately apparent in the NRSV translations. The phrase translated "physical infirmity" in Galatians 4:13 is literally "weakness of the flesh." Both of those terms are significant in 2 Corinthians 12:7–10: "flesh" in 2 Corinthians 12:7 and "weakness" three times in 2 Corinthians 12:9–10.

Though within the discussion of 2 Corinthians 12:7ff. Paul considers the broader relevance of the malady in theological terms, here Paul shows no interest in what role God, Satan, or any other figure may have played in initiating, maintaining, or healing his infirmity. Rather he puts the focus squarely on the Galatians and their response. And they seem, quite literally, to have passed "the test" in a manner most impressive to Paul. So returning to Cicero, who considers the role of "trials" or "tests" in *On Friendship* 62, they have shown themselves as true friends.

The relevance of 2 Corinthians 12:7–10 may be greater in sorting out Paul's imagery herein than in determining the form of Paul's ill health. In 2 Corinthians 12:7 Paul directly associates the "weakness" in his "flesh" with "a messenger of Satan," or, perhaps better, "an angel of Satan"; the word for "messenger" and "angel" are the same in Greek. Such an understanding is consistent with other descriptions of disease and physical challenge within the New Testament (e.g., Luke 13:16 and Acts 10:37–38). But the Galatians will have none of it. Far from relating to Paul and his condition as they would an angel of Satan, they "welcomed," or "received," him as "an angel of God," even as Jesus Christ.

Paul's wording here is more than friendly overstatement. In 1 Thessalonians, Paul remembers the Thessalonians' initial acceptance of his gospel with this same verb he uses here: "you *received* the word" (1 Thess. 1:6). The Thessalonian instance throws further light on his (seemingly) passing reference to Jesus Christ. Therein, Paul writes about how they became "imitators of us and of the Lord" and in turn became "an example" for others. In that context, how could they have become "imitators of . . . the Lord" but through the teaching and example of Paul, which conveyed (the gospel of) Christ? Such description as this and such language as "apostle" in Galatians 1:1 is consistent with one who is present in Christ's stead—so the last phrase of 4:14. Within a passage quoted in the comments on 1:1, the moral philosopher Epictetus writes that the true teacher must know that he has been sent as a "messenger" (or "angel": the same word that Paul uses here) from God to humans (*Discourses*, 3.22.23). So the Galatians accepted Paul, as both "angel" and representative "of God, as Christ Jesus."

What happened? Paul's question at the top of verse 15 could not be more blunt. The actual meaning or nuance of the succint language is less clear. The complications of this verse mirror those discussed in 2:16 with regard to the meaning and usage of faith/faithfulness. Here the particular Greek word translated "good will" has a range of meaning, including "blessedness" (see Rom. 4:6, 9), "good will," or simply "happiness." The relationship of "you" Galatians to that word is ambiguous; is the "you" the subject (that is, source or owner) of the good will/blessedness, or the object (that is, receiver of whatever action or sentiment the word implies).

The NRSV translation captures the range of possibilities admirably. Paul wants to know what happened to the Galatians' initial positive reception of him and his gospel—the blessedness they felt—*or* the sense of good will that they, as source, shared with Paul. Given the remainder of verse 15, it seems likely that the latter of the two is the more likely; indicating a "blessedness" or "good will" that they shared.

There is something of a formality, certainly some rhetorical posturing, to the phrase, "I testify." The range of semantic fields that the verb engages includes the law court, testimony regarding the integrity of an individual or group, and theological statements and "witnessing" to and for God. Paul is calling the Galatians to account, based on his witness or testimony of their deep relationship to him (and by extension, his gospel).

Recalling the discussion about verse 13, does the content of the second half of verse 15 provide information regarding Paul's illness or weakness? It may. Another possibility is that here Paul is providing a turn of phrase to indicate that, consistent with the motif of true friendship, they would have sacrificed what is most precious to them on his behalf. The preciousness of the eye, or what we would call "the apple" of the eye, is known within biblical tradition (Deut. 32:10; Ps. 17:8; Prov. 7:2; Lam. 2:18; Zech. 2:8). What connection, if any, is there between the use of "eyes" in this verse and in 3:1? Presumably none, though these are the only two verses in the letter that use the word and they share the same context, the Galatians' initial reception of the gospel.

The next verse, consistent with much that we have seen in this section, sits comfortably within broader discussion around the motif of friendship. Returning to Cicero's *On Friendship*, "truth is troublesome" to friendship or, at least, can be. Cicero continues, "if someone's ears are so closed to the truth that that one is unable to hear truth from a friend," the friendship may be lost (89). That would be little comfort to Paul. This is a relationship he is fighting for within the bonds of friendship and on several other levels as well.

"Enemy" is a word that Paul may have introduced or he may be adopting it from the rival teachers' attacks against him. Martyn notes in his commentary (p. 422) that the same word appears with regard to Paul in the *Epistle of Peter to James*, which is likely a second century composition. Peter writes of those Gentiles who "have rejected my lawful preaching and have preferred a lawless and absurd doctrine of the one who is my enemy." There is little doubt that the *Epistle of Peter to James* reflects broadly and indirectly on the rift that is evident in Galatians. Does it also reflect or even preserve specific language used by one or another of the main players (including the rival teachers)?

In verse 17 Paul exhibits something of his nimble linguistic skills as well as the extent of his sense of bitterness toward the rival teachers and his perception of their agenda. Having already employed parent-child, sibling, slave, friendship, and other relationships in his rhetoric, Paul now takes a quick and somewhat subtle turn by extending the friendship theme to courtship. The NRSV translation, "they make much of," captures a very broad and noncontextual sense of the Greek verb, from which the English word "zealous" is derived. Paul himself uses the same word in 2 Corinthians 11:2 in a similar vein (though there in a positive sense), which the NRSV captures well: "I feel a divine jealousy for you, for I promised you in marriage. . . ." The point in Galatians 4:17 is that the rivals are courting "you" for no "good purpose." Worthy of a literary trope that ranges in our culture from literary novels to TV sitcoms (and, in Hellenistic culture, enjoys about the same range, from higher to more popular literature) their game, Paul states, is to chase after and then exclude or, better, "cut you off," for the purpose of inducing you to "make much of," or jealously desire, "them." The point for Paul is that the teachers' message smacks of exclusion and will always leave "you," Gentiles, on the outside looking in.

Now Paul does indeed turn the word positively, as he does in 2 Corinthians 11. It is "good," he writes in verse 18, to be courted or "made much of" in "good" ways—who would argue that?! In the next phrase Paul removes himself from what might have become the role of the jealous or spurned lover. Being courted—as young Christians—by Christian teachers and preachers is a good thing generally, and not just when "I am present with you." Paul's objection is not to other teachers gaining access to the community he founded.

And now Paul switches metaphors again, to that of mother, beginning with an address that is both familiar and different. The use of "children" has been evident, repeatedly, from 3:7, and its biblical roots have been discussed in comments on 3:7, 3:26, and 4:5. Here Paul addresses the Galatians directly, using a separate, etymologically unrelated term with roughly the same meaning and range of meanings. Unlike the previous term, however, this one is essentially generic—meaning "child" (sing.) and "children" (plural)—which is not to say that it lacks depth of feeling. Paul returns to it regularly in expressing the dear relationship he feels to both an individual (Phlm. 10) and groups (1 Cor. 4:14–15 and 1 Thess. 2:7; the latter is a particularly important parallel as there Paul also takes on the role of a mother).

Here the NRSV captures well Paul's use of the word "pain," nuanced by the implied context of childbirth. The use of the mother metaphor, with attendant imagery, is striking then as now, and it is one that Paul employs repeatedly, most vividly in his earliest letter (1 Thess. 2:7, as was noted above). Besides the 1 Thessalonians verse and this one, there is also the somewhat more subtle, and usually overlooked, case of 1 Corinthians 3:1–2. Who, if not Paul, as nursing mother, is the source of the milk? Paul is nothing if not a nimble and resourceful rhetorician and teacher and he seems to return to the motif of the birthing mother or mother of newborns precisely in recalling (1 Thess. 2:7, 1 Cor. 3:1–2) or facilitating (herein) the challenges of forming new communities in Christ.

Paul is also a good student of the Hebrew Bible and constantly (re)turns to that source. And so here he is likely drawing on Isaiah 45:10: "Woe to anyone who says to a father, 'What are you begetting?' or to a woman, 'with what are you in labor?'" In that text it is God who is both father and mother. The "children" of the next verse, Isaiah 45:11, are, of course, Israel. And, by the close of that chapter, "the nations" (Isa. 45:20) and "all . . . the earth" (Isa. 45:22) are within view—a theme Paul will visit shortly in the discussion of Hagar and Sarah in 4:21–31 (with its implicit allusion to Isa. 54).

These chapters toward the close of Isaiah are, generally speaking, apocalyptic, as they consider the coming time of restoration. That apocalyptic orientation is consistent with the context in which Paul generally employs the language of "labor pains" in his earliest (1 Thess. 5:3) and latest (Rom. 8:22) extant letters, which is, in turn, consistent with Isaiah (13:8) and prophetic literature more broadly (Jer. 6:24; Hos. 13:13; cf. Jesus in Mark 13:17 and par.).

Romans 8:22–23 provides perhaps the closest and most telling parallel to our passage as Paul references both "the Spirit" and "adoption," two topics that weigh heavily in this central section of Galatians (see esp. 3:1–6 and 3:29–4:7.) Consistent with the apocalyptic theme that runs throughout this letter (see above comments on 1:3–5, 12, 16, and 3:27), Paul's struggles hold meaning on at least two levels: (1) the formation of the Christian communities in Galatia and (2) the manifestation of the Spirit in forming Christian communities at the end times.

How far does one push a metaphor? Or, put another way, how far does one follow a metaphor? The close of verse 19 speaks of Christ "being formed" in or among "you." It is the only time Paul uses this verb in his extant letters. Within the immediate context of childbirth provided by the first part of the verse it would be natural, perhaps even expected, for Paul's addressees to consider the formation of an embryo inside the uterus, since this same word was used to refer to such. That being the case, the logic of the verse would be that Paul, as mother, was birthing an embryonic Christ into the metaphorical womb of "you," the community. Dare one observe that this is quite a pregnant image (?)and one that is arguably consistent with Paul's statements in verses 5:6 and 5:22 regarding that "working" or "fruit" that is to be produced by the community? Also relevant is the use of the noun "form" in the Christ Hymn wherein Christ abandons "the form of God" by "taking the form of a slave" (Phil. 2:6–7); Christ has been and can be variously "formed."

The section draws to a close with quite a clash of mood and phraseology. Following the complex, arguably endearing, and certainly expansive and hopeful metaphor of verse 20, Paul reintroduces the motif of being present (see v. 18), signaling the bond and desire he feels for the community, only to admit point-blank, at verse's end, his utter frustration with his addressees. But there is more. An important parallel in verses 19–20 is lost in the English translation since therein differing prepositions precede "you." In Paul's Greek, it is the same preposition, literally "in," which holds a range of meaning. In verse 19 Christ is being formed in/among "you" while in verse 20 Paul is "confused" or "uncertain" in/about you. That is quite a switch for Paul's addressees, the "you" on the receiving end of these words: from a nurturing womb, itself nurtured by mother Paul, in which Christ is to be formed, to an object of frustration and uncertainty.

12. Abraham and Sonship Revisited: The Cases of Hagar and Sarah
Galatians 4:21–5:1

4:21 **Tell me, you who desire to be subject to the law, will you not listen to the law?** [22] **For it is written that Abraham had two sons, one by a slave woman, and the other by a free woman.** [23] **One, the child of the slave, was born according to the flesh; the other, the child of the free woman, was born through the promise.** [24] **Now this is an allegory: these women are two covenants. One woman, in fact, is Hagar, from Mount Sinai, bearing children for slavery.** [25] **Now Hagar is Mount Sinai in Arabia and corresponds to the present Jerusalem, for she is in slavery with her children.** [26] **But the other woman corresponds to the Jerusalem above; she is free, and she is our mother.**
   [27] **For it is written,**
> **"Rejoice, you childless one, you**
> **who bear no children,**
> **burst into song and shout, you**
> **who endure no birth pangs;**
> **for the children of the desolate**
> **woman are more numerous**
> **than the children of the one**
> **who is married."**

[28] **Now you, my friends, are children of the promise, like Isaac.** [29] **But just as at that time the child who was born according to the flesh persecuted the child who was born according to the Spirit, so it is now also.** [30] **But what does the scripture say? "Drive out the slave and her child; for the child of the slave will not share the inheritance with the child of the free woman."** [31] **So then, friends, we are children not of the slave but of the free woman.** 5:1 **For freedom Christ has set us free. Stand firm, therefore, and do not submit again to a yoke of slavery.**

As if gathering a second wind, Paul launches another extended argument (4:21–5:1) and final statements against circumcision for Gentile converts to Christian community (5:2–6) and against the rival teachers (5:7–12), before moving into the hortatory or pastoral sections of the letter

(5:13–6:10). Interestingly, the imperative form—used for commands or demands—is employed at the beginning of two of these subsections, 4:21 and 5:2. Paul is quite literally calling his addressees to—even demanding that they—take stock of his arguments and his position, lest they turn to the rival teachers and their agenda and understanding of the gospel. Charles Cousar, in this descriptive phrase, notes well that Paul's "rhythm of arguments between intimate appeals (3:1–5; 4:12–20) and lengthy exegetical discussions (3:6–4:7, 21–31) aim at both experience and reason, at the heart and the head" (pp. 95–96). Yes. And these come to a head in this section; indeed Cousar might have added 5:2–12, which shows many parallels to 3:1–5, to the short list of "intimate appeals."

Paul begins in a familiar place, with the phrase "subject to the law." This is the same language Paul has used repeatedly in 3:23, 25, and 4:4–5 in order to describe and argue for the state from which Christians—*all* Christians, Jewish *and* Gentile—are freed in Christ. Paul's language is simple and consistent: that which the NRSV renders variously as "subject to" or "under" is in Paul's language herein always "under." Clearly to "desire" such bondage or subjection is unfathomable, and just as Paul has repeatedly dipped into Scripture to build his case, so he will again. We have already seen that Paul's use of "law" can be, at times, hard to pin down and even quite expansive (see, e.g., comments on 4:4–5). Here he veers again, employing "law" in a sense quite familiar within contemporary Judaism, though different than that which he has employed thus far in Galatians, to refer to Scripture, and specifically to the books of Moses.

Complicating the matter, and adding further nuance, is that Paul does not appear to quote directly from the Genesis accounts of Abraham, Hagar, and Sarah (at least, not as we have them in extant versions of the Hebrew Bible or Septuagint), but appears to draw from tradition and his own summations of Genesis 16:15; 21:2–3, 9 (though see the comment below regarding vv. 22–23, Paul's use of "slave-girl").

Paul's use of "flesh" and "promise" in verse 23 (cf. "flesh" and "Spirit" in v. 29) has been set up well by his previous use of these terms (2:20; 3:3, 16–19, 21–22, 29). Indeed, there is a creative tension within his treatment of these terms thus far, as alluded to in the comments on 2:20 above, in that Paul's paradigmatic life "in the flesh" is centered on "the Son of God" and specifically Christ's justifying death (2:20–21), not in the works of "the law," a central component of which—clearly in the rivals' teachings—involves Gentile Christians undergoing fleshly circumcision.

The other contrast introduced here is also familiar due to Paul's rhetoric and teaching thus far: slave versus free (cf. 4:1–7). That said, in verses

22–23 Paul switches from the broadly used (in the Bible and in contemporary philosophical and legal discourse) word group for "slave" and "slavery" to the particular term for "slave-girl" that is employed regarding Hagar in the Septuagint version of Genesis 16:1–3, 6, 8. Also of interest, Paul tellingly swaps the technical term for "bear," which is used consistently in the Septuagint regarding Hagar (16:2) and Sarah (21:2–3), and instead opts for another verb for "giving birth," which he uses elsewhere in his letters for "bearing" Christian communities (1 Cor. 4:14–15; Phlm. 10). In light both of the mothering language he has just employed (4:19) and the texts just cited, there is little doubt that this switch, deliberate or not, is meaningful for Paul and perhaps also for his addressees: discussion of "giving birth" to Christian communities may well have been part of Paul's initial missionary preaching and teaching (see comments on 4:19, above).

In verse 24 Paul begins to spell out in no uncertain terms what would be outrageous to the ears of the rival teachers and to Paul's fellow Jews generally—the connection among Hagar, Sinai (law), and slavery. And, of course, it is because of the rivals that Paul makes the argument. His point here, as we've seen throughout Galatians, is not a Christian versus Jewish one but has to do with what will be the way forward for engaging Gentiles into the gospel message and into Christian community.

Paul's bald statement here regarding "two" covenants is telling and recalls directly his wrestling with the notion of "another" or "different" gospel at the top of the letter (1:6–7). For Paul, as we have seen (3:6–18 and, more broadly, 3:6–4:7), the covenant—*the* covenant—is that "ratified by God" with Abraham (3:17), and its crucial point, at least for Paul, is that "God would justify the Gentiles by faith" (or by "[Christ's] faithfulness"; see comments on 3:8). Since that cannot be annulled (3:15), there can be no doubt that Paul will settle on one of these two covenants, and that it will coincide with his one gospel.

It should be noted that the use of "covenant" here is pointedly different than in 3:15 where, as indicated in the comments above, the NRSV rightly understands Paul to be referring to an individual's last will and testament and, via notation, marks the word for "will" as being the same word for "covenant." Here Paul is employing the term in its technical, scriptural sense, rendering his argument all the more profound. Because the same Greek word is used in both 3:15 and here, Paul's addressees would more closely connect the two verses than we can connect them in English translation.

By way of walking his addressees through the argument, Paul wants to be crystal clear that "this" biblical, traditional, as-told-by-Paul story of two women and their offspring is "an allegory." This is the only actual use of the term "allegory" within the New Testament, which is not to say that the practice of allegory is not employed elsewhere. Within another of his letters, Paul provides a kind of primer of how allegory can and did work for teachers, Gentile and Jewish, in the Hellenistic world. For example, in a discussion of the Passover meal, Paul exclaims, "let us celebrate the festival." That by itself is an interesting statement in light of our letter and telling for those who would remove Paul from Judaism or understand his arguments in Galatians to be willy-nilly against Jewish practices. He says to celebrate Passover not with the "old yeast . . . of malice and evil"; rather, with the "unleavened bread of sincerity and truth" (1 Cor. 5:7–8; see also 9:8–10). For Paul, as one using allegory to interpret, it is not about the bread or the leaven or even, simply, the celebration; more is at stake and there is more going on than a surface understanding would indicate. Interestingly, the most prolific allegorist among Jews, and perhaps among all writers—Gentiles included—contemporary with Paul, was Philo of Alexandria. He, like Paul in 1 Corinthians, famously understands Jewish festivals to be all about ethical and philosophical truth *and* also, against some allegorists, favors practicing celebrating the festivals in the traditional way (Philo, *On the Migration of Abraham*, 79–83). Philo also, though in ways different than Paul, turns to Sarah and Hagar to mine their stories for allegorical truths (*On Mating with the Preliminary Studies*, 23; see also *On the Posterity and Exile of Cain*, 130 and *On the Change of Names*, 255).

There is no doubt that Paul is reacting to the rival teachers' understanding of covenant and, perhaps, their own use of the Hagar and Sarah narratives. For Paul a full welcoming of Gentiles into Christian community does not include circumcision and to force or promote circumcision is to promote religious bondage (3:22, 3:28–4:7). That has been the thrust of Paul's argument through the heart of the letter.

And so Paul understands Hagar, the slave, to represent not "Sinai" or Jewish law per se, but the rivals' and others' use of Jewish law for and within Christian mission. And here again Paul's swapping out of the Septuagint word for "bearing" children in favor of his own pointed use, which has to do with founding Christian community, is relevant (see comments on vv. 22–23 above). The rivals (= Hagar) are "bearing children for slavery"; that is, the rivals are promoting a sense of mission and community that does not serve the goal of freedom in Christ.

What can verse 25 possibly mean? Paul is carrying through on his agenda as spelled out in verse 24. Hagar "is," by way of allegory, Sinai or Jewish law, and that corresponds with "the present Jerusalem." Indeed! Paul has made that crystal clear in the narrative portion of this letter, outlining both his and the opposing position (1:13–2:14; see esp. 2:12). What is important to notice is that Paul is using "Jerusalem" as shorthand to refer to the Christian church and mission based in Jerusalem, which is led by James. Such shorthand is repeated throughout Galatians (1:17–18; 2:1) and Paul's letters more broadly (1 Cor. 16:3 regarding the "gift to [the church in] Jerusalem"; similarly Rom. 15:24–26, 30–31). By way of analogy to our times, Paul's use of "Jerusalem" is equivalent to those concerned with Roman Catholic policy referring to "Rome." With that in place, Paul then refers in verse 26 to "the Jerusalem above." It is the only use of that particular language in the New Testament, but the concept is not unfamiliar in Paul's writings. In Philippians 3:20 Paul writes, "our citizenship is in heaven." Even more telling, the context is apocalyptic; Philippians 3:20 continues, "and it is from there that we are expecting a Savior, the Lord Jesus Christ."

Here too Paul draws both directly (in the Isaiah quotation to follow) and indirectly on the apocalyptic. First, "the other woman" is, of course, Sarah, who represents the other covenant, *the* covenant that drives Paul's gospel and drives his argumentation in this letter. Paul's own relationship with that gospel is not via any human institution but via "revelation," from Jesus Christ above (1:12). Second, Paul is drawing on broad traditions regarding both the heavenly Jerusalem and Abraham. Regarding the former, Revelation 21, most of which is given over to description of "the new Jerusalem, coming down out of heaven" (21:2), draws on many biblical motifs. In verses 12–13 we learn of the city's gates, open and welcoming, to all four directions (north, south, east, and west). In verse 24 we hear that "the nations will walk by its light." That motif of a tent open on all four sides and welcoming others in is also consistent with Jewish midrashic (interpretive) tradition regarding Abraham and Sarah (*Genesis Rabbah* 48.9).

Such an apocalyptic orientation (see also comments above on 4:19) is consistent with that which Paul finds in Isaiah 54:1 and in chapter 54 of Isaiah generally. Paul quotes 54:1 in full here. Read within the allegorical framework that Paul has introduced, this Scripture from Isaiah tells us that "our mother" Sarah, who is "free" and who corresponds with Paul's non-Jerusalem based, non-circumcision gospel, will bear children "more numerous" than the rivals' Jerusalem-based, circumcision gospel. Indeed, the very next verse in Isaiah instructs, "enlarge the site of your tent, and let the curtains of your habitations be stretched out," so great will be the expansion. That is the promise that the rivals are simply missing, and that Paul holds out for the Galatians.

Consistent with the note in the NRSV and consistent with the language of birth and family that runs through this section and chapter 4, Paul addresses "you" Galatians as his "brothers" or "siblings" in verse 28. Hagar's son, Ishmael, goes unnamed, though not untreated (see v. 29) herein, while the allegorical children of Sarah are indeed tied to "Isaac." When turning to the famous biblical story of Ishmael's mistreatment of Isaac (Gen. 21:9), Paul uses the term "persecuted" to describe the interaction between the two boys. Such is consistent with discussion of that text in Jewish tradition (*Genesis Rabbah* 53; cf. Josephus, *Antiquities*, 1.215) and apparently describes Paul's fears and knowledge of harassment or threat that the Galatians are under from the rival teachers (cf. 5:11 regarding Paul). Indeed, the use of "now" points to the source of the harassment or threat, because it is the same word in Greek that Paul uses in labeling "the *present* Jerusalem" (emphasis mine), which is presumably the base of the rivals' mission.

The Spirit language of verse 29 underscores much that we have seen throughout Paul's argument, beginning in earnest in 3:3, while the quotation of Genesis 21:10 in verse 30 recalls the "inheritance" language of 4:7. Given the guidelines (v. 24), statements and arguments beginning from verse 21 to this point, verse 31 hardly needs stating. That said, it draws on the language of verse 28 directly ("brothers/siblings," "children") with a twist: "you" has now become "we"; a reprisal of the pronoun switching Paul established earlier in chapters 3 and 4 (see esp. comments on 3:14, above) as well as a simple and profound modeling of his statements in 3:28 and 4:6–7.

In his commentary, Hans Dieter Betz is clear that the "exhortation" or hortatory portion of the letter begins with "an abrupt new start" in 5:1. The paragraph break in the NRSV, which follows 5:1, suggests a start to the hortatory section either at 5:2 or at 5:13, which also follows a paragraph break. In his commentary, J. Louis Martyn favors placement of the beginning of the hortatory section of the letter at 5:13. As indicated in the brief introduction to this section above, such is the understanding here.

That the scholarly community experiences great difficulty in locating the boundary between the final arguments of the central section of the letter and the hortatory section that begins to bring the letter to a close, is perhaps a tribute to the "rhythm of arguments" in Paul's rhetoric discussed in the brief introduction to this section. For example, even though I would put 5:1 and 5:13 in distinctly separate sections of the letter, I would not hesitate to see the connection between Paul's use of "freedom" in both—the latter followed by the command "do not. . . ." In 5:1, the double punch of "freedom . . . set us free" is followed by a double command: "stand firm . . . do not submit again to the yoke of slavery."

What is Paul's agenda in 5:1? For Betz the imperative, "stand firm," "sets up the ethical consequences of liberation through Christ . . . " (Betz, 1979, 257). That is to miss the thrust of the whole of 3:1–5:12. Paul's focus is still unremittingly on the rival teachers and their influence on the Galatians. It is "for freedom"—freedom from "observing special days, and months, and seasons, and years" (4:10), freedom from "beggarly elemental spirits" (4:9), freedom from "beings that by nature are not gods" (4:8), freedom from "the law" (4:5), freedom from "elemental spirits" (4:3), freedom from "the power of sin" (3:22), freedom from "the curse of the law" (3:13), freedom from "the flesh" (3:3)—"that Christ has set us free." The "us," like the "we" in 4:31, profoundly models the understanding of the equal stature and parallel experience of Gentile and Jew that Paul has been at pains to construct (see esp. comments on 4:3). "Slavery"—as in the allegory in the present section, the summary statement of 4:7, and the list of earlier verses just cited in the previous sentence—marks a regression for the Galatians to their pre-Christian state. It also recalls Paul's descriptive language in the narrative section of the letter (2:4) in which he writes of "false believers secretly brought in" to his meetings with the leaders of the Jerusalem Christian mission, "who slipped in to spy on the freedom we have in Christ Jesus, so that they might enslave us." By way of expanding our statement about "slavery," we can say that for Paul slavery describes the individual's and the community's pre-Christian state *and* the rival teachers' agenda. That those teachers and their influence are foremost on Paul's mind throughout this section is seen in 5:2.

13. Circumcision and the Rival Teachers Revisited
Galatians 5:2–12

5:2 **Listen! I, Paul, am telling you that if you let yourselves be circumcised, Christ will be of no benefit to you.** [3] **Once again I testify to every man who lets himself be circumcised that he is obliged to obey the entire law.** [4] **You who want to be justified by the law have cut yourselves off from Christ; you have fallen away from grace.** [5] **For through the Spirit, by faith, we eagerly wait for the hope of righteousness.** [6] **For in Christ Jesus neither circumcision nor uncircumcision counts for anything; the only thing that counts is faith working through love.**

[7] **You were running well; who prevented you from obeying the truth?** [8] **Such persuasion does not come from the one who calls you.** [9] **A little yeast leavens the whole batch of dough.** [10] **I am confident about you in the Lord that you will not think otherwise. But whoever it is that is confusing you will pay the penalty.** [11] **But my friends, why am I still being persecuted if I am still preaching circumcision? In that case the offense of the cross has been removed.** [12] **I wish those who unsettle you would castrate themselves!**

There is, arguably, a problem with the title to this subsection. Neither the noun, "circumcision," nor the verb, "circumcise," appears in chapters 3 and 4. How can one revisit what has not been visited in the first place? Of course, the matter of circumcision has been named and looms large in the heart of the Letter to the Galatians. The whole of chapters 3–4 can rightly be considered an extended argument against the rival teachers' agenda of bringing Gentiles into full Christian community via circumcision and other observances of the law. Both the noun and verb are used repeatedly in chapter 2, and the naming of the "circumcision faction" (see comments on 2:12, above) toward the close of the narrative sections helps to launch Paul's extended argument in 3–4. Paul is not going to drop that argument before stating outright what he thinks and what he wants from the Galatians.

With its "Listen!" the NRSV captures something of the emphatic and somewhat unusual way that Paul marks his final arguments against circumcision. The idiomatic expression, actually an imperative form of the word for "see," is typical of Gospel narrative but unique here within Paul's letters. The emphatic "I" and the self-naming are also somewhat unusual, though not unknown, within the extant letters of Paul (see 1 Thess. 2:18; Phlm. 9). Second Corinthians 10:1 offers a close parallel both in terms of language and context as Paul, there as here, is defending himself and his "gospel" (2 Cor. 10:14) against others on the scene who are critical of him and his message in his absence (2 Cor. 10:10–11). What follows will both focus and further his message to his Galatian addressees.

Seizing all authority that he has built up within the community, Paul declares to his addressees, by way of a theoretical conditional sentence, "should you circumcise" (my translation), then "Christ will be of no benefit to you." The first part of the condition, as indicated by the simple "should" phrase, and somewhat less clearly by the NRSV's "if" clause, follows the grammatical formula for a simple condition contrary to fact. That is, the clear presumption behind the condition, simply from a grammatical standpoint, is that it has not happened; that is, the Galatians have not undergone circumcision. The second part of the condition states clearly what is insinuated throughout chapters 3 and 4 and worked out by way of allegory in 4:24, 30. Accepting the "covenant" (4:24)—or is it, on some level, a "different gospel" (see 1:6)?—would remove the Galatians from the sphere of Christ; they would be signing on to a mission and an agenda that is not consistent with God's action through Christ and is inconsistent with established Christian mission practice (2:3, 7–10). To make the point Paul introduces a simple word for "benefit" familiar in various spheres of intellectual, moral, and social life (cf. Rom. 2:25).

And "again," in verse 3, Paul circles back to make a similar point. That Paul has in fact not made this same statement previously in the letter seems beside the point, even given the "again," since the thrust of his argumentation, as well as specific statements (see 3:10–12), would lead to this conclusion. It is interesting that the closest parallel to this statement within Paul's letters is found in an extended discussion in Romans 2:25–29, the first verse of which uses the same word for benefit employed in verse 2 here.

Using "testify" is particularly fitting for Paul, a trained Pharisee (see discussion of 1:13–15, above), since the Greek word, from which we derive our word "martyr," has at its root to do with bearing witness to something that one has seen or otherwise experienced and knows to be true. That said, there was no one Pharisaic take on the complex of matters that Paul's statement encompasses, including circumcision of Gentile converts to Judaism, expectations of the extent to which such converts would keep the law, and—even more broadly—expectations around how anyone, Jews included, would keep the law. Clearly these matters are up for debate in extant Rabbinic literature. Among the many recorded stories one could turn to is the famous one about the rigorist, unwelcoming (to a would-be convert) Shammai and the welcoming, seemingly lenient (though challenging in other ways) Hillel. Therein Hillel recites something akin to the Golden Rule and equates it with the whole Law, saying that all the rest (that is, all of the regulations and codes) is merely commentary (*Shabbat* 31a; see full quote below in comments on 5:14).

Given Paul's own self-description discussed above ("... far more zealous for the traditions of my ancestors ...") one might presume that he has in his sights here a fairly rigorist orientation, one based, perhaps, on the 613 rabbinic laws or something similar. What did or would the rival teachers say to this assertion and about the matter broadly? In the comments on 1:6–7 above it is noted that whoever the rival teachers are, they are associated with Jerusalem and, by extension, with James in some way. It is interesting that a parallel statement regarding the necessity of keeping the whole of the law is made in the letter of James (2:10).

And again, Paul makes a direct statement condemnatory of the rivals' teachings and of the move that Galatians are, or might be, considering. The use of the pronouns, "you" and "we," is telling in verses 2–5, as is the way Paul frames the argument in verses 4–5 with "justified" and "righteousness." As indicated in the comments on 2:16, above, "justified" and "righteousness" are cognates; that is, in the Greek, these two words are built from the same root word. In verses 2 and 4 it is the addressees, "you," who are the subject. The statement in verse 4 is stark. Paul's language is clipped and his Greek does not include the notion of "want," which tends to find its way into English translations, such as the NRSV. Simply, "whoever is justified by the law" (my translation), "you ... have cut yourselves off from Christ; you have fallen away from grace." It is not splitting hairs—indeed, it is critical to understanding this letter—to note that the dichotomy for Paul is not that of Christ/law, but rather that of Christ/Justified-by-law. Paul has no problem recognizing a Christian mission among law-observant Jews (2:7); indeed he, like most Christians at the time, being Jewish, would not have been able to conceive of the notion of the observance of Jewish law as being somehow outside the realm of life in Christ. Paul does have a huge problem, evident throughout this letter, with those who would promote or demand law observance among Gentile converts to Christianity. There's the rub. The bulk of the verse amounts to a restatement and hardening of 2:16 and 21.

Verse 5 also amounts to a kind of restatement of 2:16 regarding faith and justification. But, there is more. In context, the "you," now changes to "we" and vis-à-vis 2:16 this "we" stands on the far side of 3:28 and 4:7 and surrounding arguments, rendering it perfectly clear that no marker or boundary, man-made or otherwise (see the commentary on 2:15), delimits those included among the "we." Further, it is "through" or even "in" the Spirit (see comments on 1:6) that "we" carry on together, with "the Spirit" recalling the very beginnings of formation of, and identity in, Christian community (3:1–5). The close of the verse brings something new as Paul introduces a verb, captured well by the phrase "eagerly wait for." Throughout the commentary we have noted the instance of apocalyptic themes and language (1:3, 8, 12, 16; 3:28; 4:4–5, 19, 26); so here. Consistent with its use elsewhere in Paul's letters (Rom. 8:19, 23, 25; 1 Cor. 1:7; Phil 3:20), the verb points and orients Paul's addressees to a future, full experience of "righteousness." "Hope," most familiar in Romans 8:18–39 and 1 Corinthians 13:13 among passages in Paul's letters, is also introduced into the letter here.

Both of these words, "hope" and the verb translated "eagerly wait for," appear in Romans 8:24–25, in which hope is defined/explained. Though Paul forgoes any such explanation here, one wonders whether it was part of his initial teaching to the Galatians while present with them. The juxtaposition of "justified" and "righteousness" in verses 4–5 suggests just such an orientation. Those Christians who (wrongly) take themselves to be justified by the law (note the present tense) stand in juxtaposition to "we" who "eagerly wait for the hope of righteousness" or "justification."

That anticipatory orientation sets up and is affirmed beautifully by verse 6, the first part of which provides the content, in terms of central concern of the letter, of the inclusionary nature of the "we." While verse 5 can be understood as a kind of restatement of 2:16, here at the close verse 6 it is 2:20 that looms large. There Paul states, through the use of the paradigmatic "I," that for Christian individuals and community ". . . it is no longer I who live, but it is Christ who lives in me." And further, as discussed above, that living is accomplished "by" or through "the faithfulness of the Son of God, who loved me and gave himself for me."

Christ is both savior *and* model for the faithful life, with the emphasis here in 5:6 being on the latter. Christ embodied and modeled "faith" or "faithfulness" working through "love" and so do/might/should/could "we"; after all, it is "the only thing that counts." Challenging words, yes! But what a foundation they have (2:16–20). Though the whole of the NRSV phraseology, ". . . counts for anything; the only thing that counts . . ." is, as Paul wrote it, made up of only two words (a verb meaning "to be able," or "to have meaning," followed by a contrastive "but"), the NRSV translation rightly stresses the matter. Paul has throughout the letter and throughout his career in mission to Gentiles (2:2), been arguing for equal validity for (uncircumcised) Gentiles within Christian community. Faith(fulness) is both what forms and shapes (3:5) *and* what results (5:6) from Christian community.

In verse 7, Paul throws the spotlight back onto the rival teachers. He does so by setting the stage with a word, and a broader analogy, which he uses elsewhere in this letter (Gal. 2:2) and in other letters (Rom. 9:16; 1 Cor. 9:24, 26; Phil. 2:16): "running." Tellingly, he puts the word in the imperfect past tense in Greek, reserved for ongoing action. Paul knows, and reminds the Galatians, that as a community they were "running well" for a time. Then someone "prevented" or, perhaps even better, given the foot-race analogy, "hindered" or "held back" the Galatians. This word for preventing or holding back is one Paul favors, and uses in both his earliest extant letter (1 Thess. 2:18, wherein it is "Satan" who is the actor) and latest extant letter (Rom. 15:22) as well as elsewhere (1 Cor. 9:12, in noun form). The simple flow of events, a good and productive start to the community followed by a falling away (or threat thereof), is consistent with 3:1–5 and 4:12–18; clearly the "who" of verse 7 is the same as the "who" of 3:1 and the "they" of 4:17, and the athletic hindering here is analogous to the bewitching of 3:1 and the false lover's pursuit of 4:17 (see comments above).

Indeed, these analogues can be traced, with a twist, even further back through the letter, as is suggested by Paul's use of "the truth." In 2:5 (see also 2:14) it is Paul whose relationship with "the truth of the gospel" is threatened by "false believers" or "false siblings" (see discussion of 2:4 above). As the "false believers" are to Paul, so too are the false lovers, bewitchers, and hinderers to the Galatians. The Galatians must not submit, just as Paul did not submit on their behalf (2:5; cf. 5:1). What is at stake, for Paul, is nothing less than "the truth [of the gospel]."

The use of "obeying" in verse 7 sets up well the hortatory or ethical part of the letter that begins at 5:13, while also further accentuating what is at stake in verse 6. This is the only use of "obey" in Galatians. That said, the King James Version and other translations include it at 3:1 as part of the phrase "obey the truth" (thereby tightening the analogies and consistencies between that verse and this) on the basis that the word translated "obey" is indeed included in that Greek manuscript that had come to be dominant in the western world. By not including the phrase at 3:1, the NRSV is true to the preponderance of the manuscript evidence. The juxtaposition of "obey" here and "faith" in verses 5 and 6 is worth noting, as the range of meaning of the two words does converge to some degree (see Acts 28:24). In a real sense, Paul is saying or suggesting that the rivals' hindering (v. 7) precludes the Galatians from working faithfully (v. 6).

With verse 8 Paul reintroduces himself and his initial calling of the Galatians. The word for "calls" matches precisely that used in 1:6 and insofar as it calls his addressees back to that verse, sets up the description and judgment of 5:10 (see 1:7) and the ethical injunctions beginning in 5:13. The saying in verse 9 is consistent with other contemporary Hellenistic writers in its negative connotation, and is akin to the familiar bit of folk wisdom, in our idiom, "one rotten apple spoils the whole bunch" (see also 1 Cor. 5:6). What is interesting for those familiar with the New Testament to note is that Jesus' use of similar sayings at times goes against standard, contemporary usage by casting the leavening in a positive light. (For example, in the Gospel of Matthew compare 13:33 with 16:6, 11, as well as with the narrator's comment in 16:12.)

Whether by coincidence or perhaps even by repeating words or phrases that he had shared with the Galatians directly while in their presence, Paul introduces two words/phrases that occur only once here in Galatians, but are regularly used by him elsewhere: "think" (see esp. Phil. 1:7; 2:2, 5; 3:15, 19; 4:1, 10), and "in the Lord" (used frequently in Rom., 1 Cor., Phil., 1 Thess., and Phlm.). Within Philippians, this particular word for "think" is used to organize or define Christian community around the action of and model of Jesus Christ (Phil. 2:2, 5). Indeed, in Philippians 4:2, "think" and "in the Lord" are used together.

The phraseology here leaves matters a bit ambiguous: "you will not think otherwise." Otherwise than what? Given that verses 8–9 do not provide any antecedent, the object or manner of thought must be found in verse 7 ("truth") or verse 6 ("faith . . ."). Though the regular rules of grammar would dictate the closest, so v. 7, there is little need to be concerned with precision since the two verses complement each other and are consistent. An exact parallel for "confident in the Lord" occurs in Philippians 1:14. Within the context of Galatians, "in the Lord" might be heard in light of the same verse, 2:20 (which was considered in the comments on 5:5–6), "the life I now live in the flesh" has everything to do with "faith/ faithfulness" that is both modeled by Christ and "in" Christ.

In the second part of verse 10, Paul names the rival teachers without naming them by using the very description of them and their teaching and tactics included in 1:7: "but there are some who are confusing you and want to pervert the gospel of Christ." Interestingly, the construction in 5:10 is in the singular (not the plural of 1:7). Why? For Martyn, this indicates a particular focus on the rivals' leader. That is possible. The sentence as a whole is a bit more complex than that which appears in the NRSV. A more literal translation would be, "the one who is disturbing you will bear the judgment, whoever it might be." Though the judgment itself is clear and stark, the target is left unnamed. Why? In his commentary, Betz offers an explanation, "so as not to give free publicity to the opposition," (Betz, 1979, 268 and 49 n. 65) by citing Ignatius, Bishop of Antioch, who wrote 50–60 years after Paul: "[my opponents'] names, since they are unbelievers, I have decided not to write down" (Ignatius, *To the Smyrnaeans*, 5:3).

Verse 11 ties Paul's plight to the Galatians, as it recalls 4:29 which, by way of analogy, indicates that the Galatians are being "persecuted" in some manner by the rival teachers. Is the conditional here, the "if" phrase, hypothetical or is Paul countering a rumor or report of some kind that he—even he (!)—is "still preaching circumcision"? It is difficult to imagine a scenario wherein the rival teachers were both spreading a rumor that Paul had now come to their side and were still, in some manner, "persecuting" him. Presumably what is lost for us was known to his addressees. Whatever, as a whole the verse provides a teachable moment and one familiar elsewhere in Paul: the preaching that he advocates and practices is an "offense" (literally, in Greek, "stumbling block," from which the English word "scandal" derives) because of its focus on "the cross" (see esp. 1 Cor. 1:23).

Verse 12 employs a rough synonym of the verb for "confusing" in 10b, with a significant difference. Here, Paul uses the plural form, captured by the NRSV "those." Needless to say, his words are graphic and unkind, indicative of the deep disagreement with the rivals' platform and frustration with the Galatians' entertainment of the same that has marked the letter from the first verses. The "wish" here has a parallel, though not exact, in a passing comment in Philippians 3:2. One might be tempted to respond to Paul with the witticism, "Tell us how you really feel." Besides the obvious invective, adding further bite to the rhetoric is the prohibition of Deuteronomy 23:1 looming in the background.

14. Freed to Love: A Call to Life in Community
Galatians 5:13–15

5:13 **For you were called to freedom, brothers and sisters; only do not use your freedom as an opportunity for self-indulgence, but through love become slaves to one another.** [14] **For the whole law is summed up in a single commandment, "You shall love your neighbor as yourself."** [15] **If, however, you bite and devour one another, take care that you are not consumed by one another.**

In the introduction to the previous section and in the comments on 5:1, we have seen that students of this letter have wrestled in determining just where the hortatory section begins—5:1 and 5:13 being the commonest choices. This study opts for the latter. As stated above, the focus on the rival teachers remains intact through 5:12. Now Paul's gaze turns more fully, and in a sustained way, to the community itself.

That is not to say that Paul has not been interested in, or offered advice or guidelines for, community life prior to this point in the letter. Of course that is not the case, and Paul creatively connects much in this section with what has gone before. Such is important to observe, given a history of scholarship that has at times missed those connections (see Barclay, *Obeying the Truth*, esp. 9–16) and missed Paul's own two-pronged goal of countering the rivals and reconstituting Christian community at Galatia around his understanding and presentation of the gospel (1:6–7).

Verse 13 stands as a kind of reprisal of much of chapters 3 and 4. The terms "freedom" and "slaves" jump out right away, but there is more. "Self-indulgence," as indicated in the footnote in the NRSV, is a peculiar translation of the Greek term, which is familiar in Galatians and generally translated as "the flesh." The address, "brothers and sisters," too, is familiar from earlier in the letter, as is the formative description of being "called." And then there is "love." It is not used often in Galatians but is clearly central for Paul's understanding of life in Christ (5:6; see comments there regarding also 2:20).

From early on (see comments on 1:10) we have noted a dissonance in Paul around the use of "slavery." Often, and as recently as 5:1, "slavery" is used in no uncertain terms to characterize the opposite of the Christian life, which is associated by Paul with the rivals' teachings. But, as Paul has already established, he can be nimble in his use of the "slave" metaphor. And under the banner of "Christ" (1:10) or "love," "slave" stands as a positive metaphor for life together (cf. Jesus' teaching in Mark 10:43–45 and parallels).

"Freedom" also recalls 5:1, but without the dissonance of the varied use of slavery metaphor. In 5:1 Paul's naming of "freedom" as definitive of community purpose leads outward to a renewed focus on the rivals. Here "freedom" leads inward to the broad concern sustained throughout this section of how to act toward "one another" (compare "one another," 5:13 with "all," 6:10).

That the orientation for Christian action is marked as being "through love" is no surprise in light of 2:21 and 5:6. As we have seen, particularly in comments on the latter, Christ as both savior and model is definitive of "faith [or faithfulness] working through love" and sets the agenda for what "counts" in and for Christian community. As we have already seen in 2:16 and 2:20, Paul can be very nimble and creative in his use of "flesh." Most recently, in 4:29, it is clear via the allegory that "flesh" has to do with the rivals and their teachings. Here, akin to 2:20, Paul's use of "flesh" moves more in the direction of referencing the human condition in which life, including the Christian life, is lived. In that sense the NRSV's "self-indulgence" captures well the juxtaposition of "love" contrasting with opportunities or indulgences that might influence human behavior. But that said, coming immediately on the heels of the scathing "wish" of verse 12, the association of "flesh" with the rival teachers cannot be far afield.

And the whole of the verse, and the whole section, is set up by recalling that "you" Galatians "were called." Just five verses earlier Paul uses this same language to describe himself and his first teaching and preaching to the Galatians. And 1:6 looms large here, as Paul is summing up (5:6) and focusing on life together around the gospel.

Verse 14 is fascinating in light of Jesus' teaching (Matt. 22:39 and parallels), Paul's Pharisaic experience, and contemporary Jewish writings. In comments on 5:3, wherein it is noted that there was significant latitude within Pharisaism on interpretation and application of Jewish law, a particular story regarding Rabbis Hillel and Shammai is referenced. Within that story, Hillel's position is summarized thusly: "What is hateful to you, do not to your neighbor. That is the whole Law" (*Shabbat* 31a; quoted by Martyn, 515). The close parallel with Paul's statement here (and with Jesus') cannot be missed. That said, the wording of the so-called Golden Rule that Paul uses here would seem particularly apt for Paul, as "love" (the same word is used in the Septuagint version of Lev. 19:18) is the hook into 5:13 (and beyond that, 5:6).

Is Paul here fighting fire with fire, in the sense of giving the Galatians what they seem to want—some "law" to live by? Is he establishing a "Law of Christ" (Gal. 6:2; cf. 1 Cor. 9:21)? Interesting, too, is the juxtaposition of "Spirit" which appears shortly hereafter (5:16; cf. Rom. 8:2, on "the law of the Spirit"). "Love" is the hallmark "through" (5:13) which action is to come.

And what is the alternative? Well, the one presented conditionally in verse 15—with an "if"—suggests a dog fight or beast fight. It may be relevant that Paul references "dogs" in writing about those to "beware of" in Philippians 3:2. That parallel—which includes similarly crass language regarding botched acts of circumcision (compare the final statement of Phil. 3:2 with Gal. 5:12)—would be tighter if it were clear that verse 15 had anything directly to do with the rival teachers. Second Corinthians 11:20 suggests that it may. There Paul paints a picture of the community capitulating to another's influence using both the language of slavery and of beasts: "For you put up with it when someone makes slaves of you, or preys upon you. . . ." The word in 2 Corinthians 11:20 translated "preys upon" and the word in Galatians 5:15 translated "devour" is the same Greek word.

It is also relevant that Paul, who is very possibly writing this letter from Ephesus, elsewhere states, presumably figuratively, that he himself has "fought with wild animals at Ephesus" (1 Cor. 15:32). There are parallels in contemporary pagan literature (Plutarch, *Against Coletes* 1124E) for using such language regarding human behavior; clearly Paul's language in Galatians is consistent with that. Whether or not he has in view the rivals and their (potential) influence is unclear, but the connections between this and earlier sections of the letter evidenced in 5:13–14 and the parallels of 2 Corinthians 11:20 and Philippians 3:2 render it possible that Paul is suggesting that such beast-like behavior may be fostered by the continued outside influence of the rivals.

15. Freed for Life in the Spirit
Galatians 5:16–6:10

5:16 **Live by the Spirit, I say, and do not gratify the desires of the flesh.** [17] **For what the flesh desires is opposed to the Spirit, and what the Spirit desires is opposed to the flesh; for these are opposed to each other, to prevent you from doing what you want.** [18] **But if you are led by the Spirit, you are not subject to the law.** [19] **Now the works of the flesh are obvious: fornication, impurity, licentiousness,** [20] **idolatry, sorcery, enmities, strife, jealousy, anger, quarrels, dissensions, factions,** [21] **envy, drunkenness, carousing, and things like these. I am warning you, as I warned you before: those who do such things will not inherit the kingdom of God.**

[22] **By contrast, the fruit of the Spirit is love, joy, peace, patience, kindness, generosity, faithfulness,** [23] **gentleness, and self-control. There is no law against such things.** [24] **And those who belong to Christ Jesus have crucified the flesh with its passions and desires.** [25] **If we live by the Spirit, let us also be guided by the Spirit.** [26] **Let us not become conceited, competing against one another, envying one another.**

6:1 **My friends, if anyone is detected in a transgression, you who have received the Spirit should restore such a one in a spirit of gentleness. Take care that you yourselves are not tempted.** [2] **Bear one another's burdens, and in this way you will fulfill the law of Christ.** [3] **For if those who are nothing think they are something, they deceive themselves.** [4] **All must test their own work; then that work, rather than their neighbor's work, will become a cause for pride.** [5] **For all must carry their own loads.**

[6] **Those who are taught the word must share in all good things with their teacher.**

[7] **Do not be deceived; God is not mocked, for you reap whatever you sow.** [8] **If you sow to your own flesh, you will reap corruption from the flesh; but if you sow to the Spirit, your will reap eternal life from the Spirit.** [9] **So let us not grow weary in doing what is right, for we will reap at harvest time, if we do not give up.** [10] **So then, whenever we have an opportunity, let us work for the good of all, and especially for those of the family of faith.**

The first imperative in the hortatory or ethical section of the letter is "become slaves" (5:13; one word in the Greek), and the second, found here in verse 16, is "live." Paul gives it a bit of build-up with the rhetorical flourish "I say," which precedes the imperative in the Greek text. The Greek verb Paul uses, and translated in the NRSV as "live," means, literally, "walk." The NRSV translation reflects the use of this verb in Hebrew Scripture (e.g., Prov. 8:20), contemporary Jewish writing (e.g., Philo, *On Mating with the Preliminary Studies*, 87), contemporary pagan moral philosophy (e.g., Epictetus, *Discourses*, 1.18.20), and regularly in Paul (Rom. 6:4; 8:4; 13:13; 14:15; 1 Cor. 3:3; 7:17; 2 Cor. 4:2; 5:7; 10:2, 3; 12:18, Phil. 3:17, 18; 1 Thess. 2:12; 4:1, 12; only here in Galatians), to indicate how an individual or group should conduct their life. The NRSV translations vary from text to text.

In the discussion of 5:14, above, regarding "law," Romans 8:2 was referenced. That section of Romans becomes even more relevant to 5:16 and Paul's treatment of "the Spirit" throughout this section. Recall that in 5:14 Paul states that "the law" is "summed up" or "fulfilled" (as the NRSV translates the same word in Rom. 8:4 and elsewhere). That verse follows 5:13 in which Paul mentions "freedom" twice. Now in verse 16 Paul commands his addressees to "live" or "walk" "by the Spirit . . . and do not gratify the desires of the flesh." Listen to these words from Romans 8:2–4:

> For the law of the Spirit of life in Jesus Christ has set you free from the law of sin and of death. For God has done what the law, weakened by the flesh, could not do . . . , so that the just requirement of the law might be fulfilled in us, who walk not according to the flesh but according to the Spirit.

As noted in the discussion of 5:13 gauging Paul's use of the word "flesh" in Galatians is no easy matter. Does it reference more particularly the rivals and the attention that their teachings give to works of the law including circumcision, or does it reference more so the human condition, including human frailties? Which is it in 5:16?

Though one need be very careful not to equate Paul's treatment of "the law" in Romans with that in Galatians (they are different letters written at different times to different addressees regarding different circumstances and topics), these verses in Romans, laced with several of the same terms and phrases in our section, may provide some insight and may even elucidate—given the high coincidence of phraseology—something of the content of Paul's gospel. The "flesh," whatever the immediate context—the rivals' teaching about the law, the human condition broadly, or some other immediate challenge—is not to be relied on. The Spirit, on the other hand, is of a piece with life in community in "Jesus Christ" (Gal. 3:1–2). The Spirit provides the possibility for, and the community provides the opportunity for, fulfilling that law which is later described as "the law of Jesus Christ" (6:2).

"Flesh" and "Spirit" are "opposed to each other . . . " (v. 17). The dualism is clear, as is the characterization of "these" as competing, impersonal forces that are outside of, or beyond, the individual or, better, the group; throughout this section as throughout the whole of the letter, Paul is addressing "you" Galatians as a plurality. While Romans 8:2–4 appears to provide something of a consistent parallel to Galatians 5:16, Romans 7:15–23, which has been recognized as parallel to Galatians 5:17 (see Betz), actually stands in bold contrast on a couple of important levels. First, in Romans 7 Paul treats the matter in terms of individual action and the individual's will; second, however one understands the competing forces, they are in Romans 7 cast as internal. Paul's use of "opposed to," in concert with recurring apocalyptic motifs throughout the letter, at the very least hints at an end-time scenario (cf. 2 Thess. 2:4, "opposes").

The NRSV closes out verse 17 with the words "to prevent you from doing what you want." Though somewhat ambiguous, the sense of the NRSV translation is that these forces oppose each other *for the purpose of* preventing. The Greek construction on which the translation is based can indeed indicate purpose. If Paul is indicating purpose, then one might ask him, who or what set that purpose or goal? No answer is apparent. On the other hand, the construction that Paul uses can alternatively indicate result. Hear the difference that makes: ". . . these are opposed to each other with the result that you do not do the things you wish." That sets up well the next verse, which begins with the simple contrastive, "but if you are led by the Spirit," then that result will change. Verse 17 is best understood as indicating result, not purpose.

In contrast to 5:14, Paul now reverts to the predominant use of "law" throughout the letter. Indeed, the very word rendered here as "subject to," in the construction "subject to the law," is precisely that used repeatedly, and translated in various ways, throughout chapters 3 and 4. It is used in 3:10, 22, 23, 4:2, 4:4, and 4:5 where the NRSV translates it as "under," as well as in 3:25 and 4:21 where the NRSV translates it as "subject to," and in 4:3 where the NRSV translates it as "to." One of the instances in chapter 3 (v. 23) and each instance beginning with 4:4 (so including also 4:5 and 21) directly concerns "the law." And yet, for all of that consistency with the presentation of the law in chapters 3 and 4, Paul seemingly abandons the law and returns to a broad consideration of "flesh" in verses 19–21. Why?

Paul has already established the close tie between "[the rivals' understanding and promoting of the] law" and "flesh" (e.g., 4:23, 29; also, 4:17). Second, a glance again at Romans 8:2–4 would indicate another of Paul's agenda items: in order for the community to put itself in position (cf. "might" in Rom. 8:4) to "fulfill" the law (Rom. 8:3; Gal. 5:14) it would do well *not* to do the sorts of things listed in 5:19–21. Such behaviors are associated with "flesh" (Rom. 8:3; Gal. 5:16, 17, 19). Rather, "by contrast," the community is to carry on in the manner indicated, and contra-indicated, in 5:22–25.

The lists of vices and virtues in 5:19–23 would resonate with anyone familiar with basic or popular teachings of moral philosophy from at least the time of Plato (e.g., *Republic* 7.536A; see also *Gorgias* 525A) and Aristotle (e.g., *Nicomachean Ethics*, 2.6.15–3.7.15). Epictetus, a contemporary of Paul's whose work has been considered in earlier comments, employs such lists (e.g., *Discourses*, 3.20.5–6). They are familiar as well within Second Temple Judaism (e.g., 4 Macc. 1:2–4, 18–27), within the Pauline corpus (e.g., 2 Cor. 6:6–7a; 12:20–21; Col. 3:5–8, 12; Titus 1:7–8), and in other Christian literature both within the New Testament (e.g., Jas. 3:13–18) and outside the New Testament (e.g., *Epistle of Barnabas*, 18–20).

The introduction to, function of, and to some degree the content of the lists resonate directly with much that Paul has introduced and argued for earlier in the letter. For example, notice the casting of the lists themselves. They are not presented as lists of do's and don'ts. Rather, as Paul presents the first list, it functions as evidence of "the works of the flesh." Since the "the works of the law" are mentioned repeatedly in the letter (2:16 [three times], 3:2, 5, 10, 12) and no other "works of . . ." constructions are employed, the immediate correlation between the two—"works of the law" and "works of the flesh"—is made, or at least suggested. That the list in verse 22ff. is introduced not as "works of the Spirit" but rather as "the fruit of the Spirit" furthers the tie between "works of the flesh" and "works of the law" (see esp. 3:2, 5 for the contrast of "Spirit" and "works of the law").

As for the content of the vice list—or better, "works of the flesh" list—it is notable that several of the items, beginning with "enmities" (v. 20) and ending with "envy" (v. 21), speak directly to life in community and the ability (or lack thereof) of the community to fulfill its mission (5:18, and the comments above); anyone who has ever played on a sports team, joined a band or drama troupe, worked in an office, or been active in a religious community could attest to the relevance of these items. Indeed, Paul features one of these terms, "factions," in a consideration of the disintegration of community and community purpose at Corinth (1 Cor. 11:19), which results in that community's inability to carry out even foundational community practice (1 Cor. 11:20).

As for the first three items in the list of 5:19–21, they are typical of Jewish polemic against Gentiles (see Martyn). Their use here, then, takes on a biting irony. Paul casts these behaviors, traditionally associated in Jewish polemic with Gentiles, as "works of the flesh"; that is, works associated with the rival teachers' understanding and promoting of "works of the law." On another level, and perfectly consistent with contemporary Jewish polemic against Gentiles, Paul uses the first two of these three terms in the hortatory section of his first letter to the Gentile community at Thessalonica (1 Thess. 4:3 and 4:7 respectively; see also the discussion of "kingdom of heaven," below). Indeed, it is no coincidence that the first term to follow this first grouping of three is "idolatry," which is clearly characteristic (from a Jewish viewpoint) of Gentiles; within a lengthy diatribe, Wisdom of Solomon directly associates the "making of idols" and "fornication" (14:12).

Consistent with that Gentile-directed focus of these first four items, the term "drunkenness" (v. 21, toward the end of the list) was used to refer to a preconversion state (cf.1 Thess. 5:7). Consistent with Paul's plea in Galatians 3:3, it suggests a call on Paul's part against backsliding. Even with such examples of the direct or indirect connections between this list and the body of the letter, it is telling that Paul closes it with a sort of throwaway phrase, "things like these." As already indicated, there is something stock about these lists; certainly the addressees will get the idea of the sorts of behaviors he is talking about.

And that said, once he has closed out the list, Paul calls the Galatians back to a specific verbal instruction—the word translated "warning" in the NRSV literally means "say beforehand" or even "predict"—likely presented in person while he was still with them. Within the letter, there is no such teaching or prediction, though the final sentence of 5:10 is consistent with, and equally dire as, this warning/prediction. First Corinthians 6:9–11 provides a significant parallel to 5:21b and to the whole of 5:19–21: several of the terms used therein are the same as or directly related to the words used in Galatians ("fornicators," "idolaters," "drunkards"); further, the phrase, "will not inherit the kingdom of God," is used (twice) in 1 Corinthians. Does this pattern—a nucleus of parallel terms (which can be expanded or supplemented with any number of other phrases) along with the attendant warning—suggest a particular component within Paul's repertoire of missionary preaching?

As already noted, the items in verses 22–23 can be compared to those in virtue lists within pagan, Jewish, other Pauline letters, and other New Testament and early Christian literature. And consistent with what we saw in the list of verses 19–21 there are in this list significant links to the body of Galatians. Clearly the lead in, with its direct reference to "Spirit," suggests as much (cf. 3:1–5). This exact term, "fruit of the Spirit," is found only here in Paul's letters, though the noun "fruit" and related verbs are found elsewhere, most notably in Romans (esp. 7:4–6, see comment on v. 24 below; also 6:21 ["advantages" in the NRSV] and 15:28 [see the NRSV alternative reading]) and Philippians (1:11, 22; 4:17 [NRSV, "profit"]); cf. Ephesians 5:9 ("the fruit of the light"). The farming imagery of 6:7 is consistent with this metaphor of "fruit."

Of the specific terms within the list, "love" (2:20 and 5:6; also 5:13) and "faith" or "faithfulness" (here translated by the NRSV as the latter; see esp. comments on 2:16 and 2:20) are the two that resonate with the body of the letter, and in particular with their use together in climactic passages regarding the action of Christ and the paradigmatic Christian, i.e. "I" (2:20), and specifically the community (5:6).

Paul's varied and, perhaps, playful use of "law" within this section is evident again at the close of 5:23. In a game of "[the rivals' understanding of] the law" (5:18) versus "the law" that Paul intends for his addressees to follow (5:14; cf. "the law of Christ," 6:2), which Paul has set up within this section, this statement would seem to presume the former. The rivals' "law" does not preclude such behavior; of course, "the law" that Paul is forwarding champions such (again, 2:20 and 5:6 regarding "love" and "faith"), as 5:24 makes clear.

The language of verse 24 is graphic and Paul employs a standard construction to indicate "those who belong to Christ" (cf. 1 Cor. 3:23 and 15:23 with 1 Cor. 1:12; see also Rom. 8:9; 2 Cor. 10:7). Though lost in English translation, the Greek construction used here is precisely parallel to that used in other phrases in which the NRSV uses "of Christ." So, for Paul's Galatian addressees, the very phrase would ring with that cluster of three "of Christ" phrases at the top of the letter: "grace of Christ" (1:6), "gospel of Christ" (1:7), and "servant" or "slave" of Christ (1:10); cf. also "the law of Christ" (6:2).

The action within the verse also calls the Galatians back to previous descriptions within the letter, particularly 2:19–20. There Paul, setting himself up as the paradigmatic, or model, Christian, writes: "For through the law I died to the law, so that I might live to God. I have been crucified with Christ; and it is no longer I who live, but it is Christ who lives in me. And the life I now live in the flesh I live by faith in the Son of God."

We have already seen how Paul's use of "flesh" can be somewhat nimble (see comments on 2:20 and 5:13). These two verses, 5:24 and 2:20, exemplify that. In 2:20, "in the flesh" suggests the human condition broadly, within which the individual Christian and Christian community carry on. Paul here broadens his presentation of "flesh" as that which is in opposition to "Spirit" (see esp. 3:3 and 4:29) by the phrase "with its passions and desires" (cf. 5:16, "desires of the flesh"). The term for "passions" is found in Paul only here and in Romans 7:5, wherein "living in the flesh" is marked by "sinful passions" that are "aroused by the law." With its direct association of "living in the flesh" and "the law," that verse from Romans shows consistency with much that we have seen in 3:1–5; 4:19–21 and within this section as a whole.

Striking in a comparison of 5:24 with 2:19–20 is the active, not passive, mode of the verb. "Those who belong to Christ" have not "died" (see also Rom. 7:4) or "been crucified" (see also Rom 6:6), but "have crucified the flesh." That active use of "crucified" is unique within Paul's extant letters, and is remarkable within the broader scope of contemporary literature. In his commentary, Betz includes the fascinating parallel of Philo, *On Dreams*, 2.213, in which "the mind" of the "passion-lover" is "crucified"; but there the human is not the actor, "God" is.

Galatians 5:25 is consistent with much that precedes (esp. 3:1–5 and 5:16, 18). The NRSV's "guided" reasonably gets at the gist of Paul's meaning here, but loses something of the flavor of the word that Paul employs, which is a technical term for marching in battle formation (Rom. 4:12 and Phil. 3:16). That Paul uses it also in his letter to Philippi, which was founded as a military colony, suggests that he is well aware of its military connotations.

In our time in the United States and the Western world in general, much scholarship has been focused on postcolonial critiques of western hegemony; among other things, the use of military words and images in the churches has come under debate (much of it very healthy and creative, given the military and other aggression associated with Christ and the Church from at least the time of the Crusades on). That said, these concerns and sensitivities ought not cloud us from Paul's usage, coming, as it did, in the context of the Roman imperial world with its strong culture of militarism and from a place, literally and figuratively, on the margins of power.

Here Paul sets up the Spirit in the role of commander or leader *and* sets up "those who belong to Christ" (5:25), that is "we" (5:26), as the corps, the pluralistic body, of those who follow. What might that have meant to a fledgling community, struggling to understand and define its identity vis-à-vis its own membership and to those outside? Military historians wax eloquent about the Roman phalanx, which was based on the principle that if the body of individuals remains tightly together, each protecting and being protected by those on either side, then the body moves forward to achieve its mission. There is no place for such things as "competing against each other" (5:26) when moving as a body. Analogously, any community that would answer its call, would do well to avoid "conceit," "envy," and the like.

Throughout this section, from the use of "you" (pl.) and "we," to the content itself, it has been clear that Paul has the whole body of believers, the community, in mind. That is reaffirmed in 6:1 with the (quite literally) familiar address—that is, it has to do with family—"brothers" (see the NRSV alternative translation) or "siblings" (for discussion, see comments on 1:2, 1:11, and 4:12; see also 2:4; 3:15, and 4:28). But there are a couple of twists.

At the close of 6:1, for the first time in the letter, Paul uses the singular form of the verb to address his readers. The NRSV captures the broad sense, but completely masks this pointed nuance at the close of verse 1: "[each one] watching yourself lest you be tempted." That sets a pattern that Paul will sustain from verses 3–8 (v. 2 returns to the plural "you"), before using "we" for his final words of exhortation (vv. 9–10).

The turn to the singular form of address at the close of verse 1 stands in creative tension with the first part of the sentence in which "you" (pl.) is clearly and emphatically stated and in which the profound relationship of the community to the Spirit and of each within the community to each other is (re)established. What accounts for this abrupt change and for the back-and-forth between plural (v. 1a), singular (v. 1b), plural (v. 2), singular (vv. 3–8), plural (vv. 9–10)? Perhaps it is set up by the use of the military metaphor in 5:25, as each assumes a role in and responsibility for the whole community under the guidance of the Holy Spirit. Certainly, concerning the Spirit, verse 1 picks up where 5:25 had left off.

And there is a twist there too. Distinct from the NRSV translation, the "Spirit" does not appear in noun form in Paul's Greek in verse 1. Rather, he uses one word (we need two in English) to conceive of the community as ones who have absorbed or received the Spirit; that is they are "Spiritual ones" (a term he uses repeatedly in 1 Cor. 2:15; 3:1; cf. 2:13; 12:1;

14:37). He then playfully and profoundly tells the manner in which the community of "Spiritual ones" treats the one found in "transgression": via a "spirit of gentleness."

The summary of the law (of Christ) in 6:2 is a throwback to 5:14. Lost in the NRSV translations, "summed up" (5:14) and "fulfill" (6:2), is that Paul uses the same word in each case; in 5:14 as a bare verb form, in 6:2 as part of compound verb, which, slightly over-translated, might mean "fulfill again" (i.e., following the directive of 5:14). In the comments on 5:14 we considered a similar summary by Hillel and by Jesus. Herein Paul veers from the biblical (see Lev. 19:18) Golden Rule to a motif from the pagan moral philosophers that Paul has visited previously in this letter: friendship. Xenophon, in *Memorabilia* 2.7.1–14, quotes no less than Socrates' saying, "it is necessary to share burdens with friends." Of course, Jesus is credited with a related maxim, though one using a different Greek verb for the central theme of carrying burdens: "Come to me, all you that are weary and are carrying heavy burdens, and I will give you rest" (Matt. 11:28).

Paul's "law of Christ" is tied not to any particular teaching of Jesus but to Christ's action on our behalf. That action and that faithfulness of Christ both justify *and* model the community's mission. As suggested by the Golden Rule and as spelled out here, "the law of Christ" has to do with bearing another's burdens. By way of contrast with Paul's statement regarding "Christ's law" in 1 Corinthians 9:21, Paul's focus here is internal, that is, on the community.

As discussed above in the comments on verse 1, a nuance lost in the NRSV translation is that verses 3–8, are directed to the individual within the community. Verses 3–5 are written with the singular verb regarding a hypothetical "certain one" (v. 3) or "each one" (vv. 4 and 5). Another matter lost in the NRSV is also important: though "pride" captures something of Paul's language here, the particular word he uses is usually translated "boast" (see 6:14 in which the verb form of this same word is indeed translated "boast"; cf. Rom. 4:2, 1 Cor. 5:6; 9:15, 16; 2 Cor. 1:14; 5:12; 9:3; Phil. 1:26; 2:16, all of which the NRSV translates with some form of "boast").

Verses 3 and 4 are tied together by content as well as by a wordplay linking "think" in verse 3 with "test" in verse 4—the words share the same first syllable in Greek. The point appears to be to focus on one's own "work" and not the "neighbor's," literally that of "the other." That is not bad advice for overcoming self-deception (5:3) and for carrying one's own weight (5:5). Interestingly, in Philippians Paul himself claims that he hopes to "boast" of the work of others (Phil. 2:16). Is this a teacher's prerogative? In 2 Corinthians, he provides others "the opportunity to boast about us"

(2 Cor. 5:12); again, one might ask, Is this a teacher's prerogative? But the focus here in Galatians is clearly community focused, and the concern is the relationship of the individual to others within the community.

Does verse 5 contradict verse 2 or (theoretically) take away the need for the directive therein? Perhaps. But there is a small, though very significant word, by which Paul directs his addressees differently. At the top of verse 5, Paul's use of "for" links the statement in verse 5 directly to verse 4 (and not verse 2). The maxim or teaching of this verse, then, is a kind of corollary of the previous: each should focus on his or her own "load," not that of another, in order to meet the "test" (v. 4) of overcoming possible deception (v. 3). As for the directive of verse 2, it remains intact.

The teaching of verse 6 is familiar going back at least to the time of the Hippocratic Oath. Many of us know the oath as the pledge of a doctor to "do no harm," but the ancient document addresses the student-teacher relationship, including the declaration that the one "who taught me this art [is] equal to my parents" and the directive "to live my life in partnership with him, and if he is in need of money, to give him a share of mine" (as quoted in Betz). What were Paul's reasons for including it here?

Insofar as verses 3–5 suggests autonomy and self-care, verse 6 stands as something of a redirection: it begins, in the Greek, with a "but," which is not indicated in the NRSV. All the responsibility that one takes for oneself within the community is well and good, but don't forget the teacher(s) who presented you the Word to begin with and who maintain your learning. Related to this point and central to the letter, the precipitating event(s) behind the letter and the great bulk of its content have to do with the rival teachers' promotion of their understanding of the full entry of Gentiles into the Christian fold via circumcision. Here Paul puts the focus on the teachers and teachings associated with him and his missionary enterprise, as if to say "don't forget them" either literally or figuratively. Given Paul's "word" order, the focus is clearly on the directive to "share" and, given the full meaning of "share," the focus is also on community or commonality. Through his pointed use of "the word," which in 1 Thessalonians 1:6 as here, indicates the first teachings that the community received, Paul calls his reader back to the "gospel" that they first received and supported.

Paul brings God back into the picture in verse 7. He does so, arguably, as a good rabbi, presenting a teaching consistent with this statement from the first chapter of the *Pirke Avot*: "be not doubtful of retribution" (*Pirke Avot*, 1.7, see Betz, 307 n. 159). Presumably the rival teachers would find little or nothing to disagree with in Galatians 6:7.

In verse 7 Paul folds a sow/reap metaphor into the already established flesh/Spirit dichotomy. Here he clearly confronts the position of the rival teachers. Indeed, the agricultural metaphor—which remains in force through verse 9—has been set up by his earlier establishment of "the fruit of the Spirit" that stands in "contrast" to "the works of the law."

The two new (to Galatians) terms/concepts that Paul introduces in verse 8, "corruption" and "eternal life," are both consistent with the apocalyptic themes that we have seen revisited throughout the letter. Corruption (cf. esp. Rom. 8:21 and 1 Cor. 15:42, 50) is characteristic of "the flesh" and by extension of the rival teachers and their understanding and promotion of circumcision and other works of the law for full inclusion of Gentiles into Christian community. Eternal life is associated with the Spirit and with Jesus' saving act and the reception of the Spirit.

The notion of "sow to," the second word being literally "into," parallels 2:16 in a notable way. As indicated in the comments on that verse, Paul forwards the notion of "believe into" Christ, which suggests an ethical or mystical engagement. Such is the case here, as is underscored by verse 9 with its affirmation and continuation of ethical action, which bookends the recasting of "eternal life" in terms consistent with the overarching agricultural metaphor (5:22, 6:7–9). And the use of "right," literally "good," in 6:9 parallels the use of "good" in 4:18; it is what the rivals do not do.

The switch to the plural and inclusive "we" in verse 9 (see discussion of 6:1, above) is confirmed by the summary statement of verse 10. The predominant focus on the individual, in the casting of the teachings from 6:1b–6:8 has been, finally, about the community. And where Paul was, apparently, loathe to parallel "works of the flesh" (5:19) with *works* of the Spirit (opting instead for "fruit of the Spirit" in 5:22), here he does use a verb form of "work." Why? Perhaps Paul is satisfied that he has now laid bare the distinctions between "flesh" and "Spirit"; that is, he has laid bare the distinctions of the rivals' understanding of the place and practice of Gentiles in Christian community (flesh) versus his understanding of the place and practice of Gentiles in Christian community (Spirit). Regardless, picking up on a summary verse from the previous section (3:5), he now directs "us" to "work for the good of all"—with no distinctions relevant to "us" or to the "all" (see 3:26–28, 4:7).

The final spotlight is given to "the family of faith" (NRSV) or literally, "the household of faith." A similar phrase, "household of God," is used in Ephesians 2:19. The parallel is relevant since the verse from Ephesians suggests no second class or distinction within "the household." But more to the point of Galatians is the second word, the descriptor. This "household" that Paul has founded and that has formed around the Spirit (3:3–4) based on the faith(fulness) of Jesus Christ (2:16) is itself a household of faith(fulness). The contrast is not faith versus works; in this verse and 5:6 Paul presumes and anticipates that the community will work. Rather, the matter has to do with formation and mission: the "household of faith(fulness)" is defined by Christ's faithfulness (2:16 and 2:16–21) and its only faithful, "working" response is through the Spirit (5:5–6), with no distinctions given or acknowledged among the members (3:26–28, 4:7).

16. Conclusion
Galatians 6:11–18

6:11 **See what large letters I make when I am writing in my own hand!** [12] **It is those who want to make a good showing in the flesh that try to compel you to be circumcised—only that they may not be persecuted for the cross of Christ.** [13] **Even the circumcised do not themselves obey the law, but they want you to be circumcised so that they may boast about your flesh.** [14] **May I never boast of anything except the cross of our Lord Jesus Christ, by which the world has been crucified to me, and I to the world.** [15] **For neither circumcision nor uncircumcision is anything, but a new creation is everything!** [16] **As for those who will follow this rule—peace be upon them, and mercy, and upon the Israel of God.**

[17] **From now on, let no one make trouble for me; for I carry the marks of Jesus branded on my body.**

[18] **May the grace of our Lord Jesus Christ be with your spirit, brothers and sisters. Amen.**

The conclusion of Paul's Letter to the Galatians is—at least it was—marked in no uncertain terms as the author apparently grabbed the stylus from his amanuensis, or secretary, and proceeded to write himself. In spite of that dramatic and physical distinction from the rest of the letter, or perhaps because of it, this conclusion is tied very closely and even emotionally with what has come before. Indeed, Paul's personal investment in inscribing his message, whether by putting his body on the line (5:17) or by putting pen to paper, could not be clearer as he circles back around one last time to confirm what his message is and is not, and leaves some parting visions for what life in community formed around Jesus Christ hearkens to and is all about.

As with the beginning of the letter (see introduction to the letter and comments on 1:6 above), one can approach the conclusion of Galatians by noting what is not here. For example, there are no names named or greetings given and no directive to "greet" with a "holy kiss." What is present is important reiteration of the thrust of Paul's arguments and concerns throughout the letter as well as some unique phraseology regarding the current circumstance and the current community in light of Jesus Christ.

Verse 11 is variously poignant and rhetorically charged in (re)gaining the addressees' attention. The well-known scholar Adolf Deissmann famously commented that Paul was apologizing for his bad penmanship (cited by Betz). Maybe. Perhaps, too, Paul's comment regarding his eyes in 4:15 is relevant; was there some physical impairment of sight rendering the physical act of writing difficult? Regardless of the applicability of any of the above, is Paul here calling his readers to the import of what is to follow? The word that the NRSV translates here as "large" can carry the sense of importance and gravitas, as is clear in its other use within the New Testament, Hebrews 7:4 regarding Melchizedek (NRSV: "see how great he is!").

The verses immediately following this introduction to the conclusion reprise the central issue of the letter as a whole, "circumcision" as a marker of entry in Christian community. They also reprise two other particular matters: (1) the rivals' agenda is bound up in their wanting "to make a good showing in the flesh" (4:16) and (2) the threat and reality of persecution "for the cross of Christ" (5:11). In 5:11 it is "the cross" which causes offense. There is nothing "except the cross" (v. 14) on which Paul would have himself and his addressees build identity, community, and mission.

Paul revisits the matter of boasting in verses 13 and 14. The rivals embody the very thing he warns against in 6:4. They "do not themselves obey the law" (see 5:3), and they look to others, the Galatians, as their basis for boasting. Meanwhile, Paul's intent for his "boasting," as for his proclamation of the gospel (1:7–8) is that it be about nothing except Christ (1:7) and, in particular, "the cross of our Lord Jesus Christ, by which the world has been crucified to me and I to the world" (6:14).

That phrase in verse 14 recalls both the central descriptions of 2:16–21 and also the somewhat obscure statement of 5:24, while paralleling neither exactly. As in the discussion of 5:24 above, the closest parallel to this verse within Paul's letters, at least regarding the passive use of the verb "crucified," might be Romans 6:6. It is quite fitting that, as noted in the alternative reading of the NRSV, the prepositional phrase in the second part of verse 14 may be translated as either "by which" or "through whom"; that is, the instrument or agent whereby "the world has been crucified to me, and I to the world" may be reckoned as either "the cross" or as "our Lord Jesus Christ." Presumably, Paul would accept either or both interpretation(s) since for him the two are inseparable.

The uses of "the world" in verse 14 should not be missed. A quick comparison of the earlier parallels would indicate that "world" assumes more or less the same place as "law" in 2:19–20 or "flesh" in 5:24. Another verse and concept within the letter is active here. In 4:3 Paul extraordinarily ties Jewish and Greek religious practice together under the umbrella of "elemental spirits of the world": could the use of "world" here be a shorthand reference to that verse and that concept? Yes. Further, the usage in verse 14, consistent with verses 2:19–20, 4:3, and 5:24, suggests an apocalyptic orientation.

If Paul's addressees need or want further indication of the apocalyptic and world-changing nature of Christ's action through the cross, they receive it in verse 15. Following a simple restatement of Paul's central argument (2:15–16) and the argument's conclusion (5:6), he introduces a new concept into the letter: "a new creation." Though the translation "a new creation is everything" is arguably an over-translation, it nicely captures the gist of his rhetoric at this point. Paul's sentence structure here is very much akin to that in 5:6, wherein the NRSV translates "the only thing that counts is. . . ." What Paul builds toward is a simple and profound statement that the only "something" is "a new creation."

The comparison to 5:6 is apt and invited by the parallel wording and sentence structure. "New creation" and "faith working through love" stand in parallel placement within these sentences. And they have a lot to do with each other. Behind both is the statement of 2:20, ". . . the life I now live in the flesh I live by faith in the Son of God" (see discussion above of 2:20 and 5:6 regarding "faith"). What do either 5:6 or 2:20 have to do with "a new creation"? Second Corinthians 5:17 may provide a direct answer: "So if anyone is in Christ, there is a new creation: everything old has passed away; see, everything has become new!" "Anyone" engaged in "faith working through love" is "a new creation." Of course, the paradox is that, seen another way, arguably nothing has changed. As in 2:20, "the life I now live" as a member of the community of those justified through the cross of Jesus Christ is still lived "in the flesh" (see discussion of 5:24, above). But then, "in Christ Jesus" the boundaries and barriers of the old world are no more (3:26–28, 4:7). All that counts is "faith working through love" (5:6; 6:15; cf. 2 Cor. 5:17).

The lead-in to Paul's short blessing in 6:16 seems to indicate as much: "as for those who will follow this rule." What rule? The rule of the "new creation" in which old boundaries don't count. The sweep of 6:15–16 and the resonances therein with 5:6 put an exclamation point on such verses as 4:9 and 3:3. Such backsliding that those verses speak against and the adoption of the rivals' platform that verses 4:9 and 3:3 presume are now unthinkable.

Paul is seeking for all his addressees to accept and follow this "rule" (6:16) of the new creation (6:15) and reject the rivals and their agenda. And so the blessing upon them parallels to a degree canonical ("Peace be upon Israel," Ps. 125:5; 128:6) and noncanonical blessings ("May the mercy of the Lord be upon Israel. . . ," *Psalms of Solomon*, 11.9, as quoted in Martyn). Moreover, the language and the flow ("upon them . . . upon the Israel of God") of Paul's blessings are similar to the language and flow of the well-known blessing of Peace of the Shemoneh Esreh 19 ("May peace . . . and mercy . . . be upon us and upon all Israel thy people," as quoted in Martyn). Because it is unclear when that blessing was actually codified, it cannot be known whether Paul borrowed directly from it. However, given Paul's own background and training in Pharisaism, there can be little doubt that he is here borrowing from one or another traditional blessings.

By way of providing content for the rule, besides that which we have considered already, Paul provides another significant element which is lost in the NRSV translation. The Greek verb, translated "follow," which precedes "this rule," is the same as that translated "guided by" in 5:25. As with all things relevant to life in Christian community, following "this rule" has to do with life in the Spirit, guided by the Spirit, with the Spirit as leader and the community as the context in and for action (so 6:1–10). The focus on the community is restated at the close of verse 16. The final "and" of the verse is best understood as explicative: it might be translated "that is" or "namely," because it explains that "those who follow" are "the Israel of God." A classic example of this use of the word normally translated "and" is 1 Corinthians 2:2, which, as here, the NRSV indeed translates "and"; substitute "namely" and see how it reads, and how much like Paul it sounds: "For I decided to know nothing among you except Jesus Christ; namely, him crucified."

The phrase, "Israel of God" here is not only unique within the letters of Paul, it is also unknown in the rest of the New Testament or in the Hebrew Bible or other Jewish writings. Paul is again engaging in outrageous and ironical shorthand to counter the rivals. How can he possibly equate the Gentile Christians with "the Israel of God?" The same way he has throughout the letter (4:7, 4:24). Is the statement triumphalist? Does Paul think that Christians will take the place of Israel? Far from it. To our ears it may sound like it, but in context it could not be and is not triumphalist. Consistent with Paul's agenda within Galatians, he is proving his point regarding the full status of uncircumcised Gentiles within Christian community. There is no such thing as Christian community separate from Judaism at this point. What Galatians 6:15 says is consistent with 4:7 and any number of verses and sections within this letter. For Paul, there is no place within the community of those centered on Christ for promoting or prioritizing Jewish status or, for that matter, identity markers of any kind; all are of the same status (3:26–28, 4:6–7) through Jesus Christ (see the discussion of 2:19, above).

In verse 17 Paul returns to the singular verb form one last time. He also returns to himself as subject one last time. Using the paradigmatic "I," Paul puts himself squarely into the story of Christ's justifying faithfulness and death and resurrection: "I have been crucified with Christ" (2:19). He goes on with a statement we have returned to repeatedly in the commentary: "And the life I now live in the flesh I live by faith in the Son of God" or, as discussed above, ". . . by the faithfulness of the Son of God" (2:20). For Paul, there is no extricating the Christian life from Christ and Christ's faithfulness.

Here again Paul's reference is personal. But is it paradigmatic? That is, is Paul setting himself up as model for the community and individuals within the community, or is he establishing himself and his status as something separate? Perhaps the best answer is yes, to both. As a subtext, he is affirming that avoidance of persecution (6:12) is what the rivals' agenda is about and so does not represent authentic Christian life in light of the gospel. Paul's agenda does represent authentic Christian life in light of the gospel.

We have little or no direct discussion of Paul's physical suffering at the hands of others within Galatians; though 5:11 may suggest as much, it is vague. For direct and detailed discussion, see esp. 2 Cor. 4:7–10, 11:24–26. Perhaps his addressees had heard something of Paul's physical struggles in his direct missionary preaching to them. Worthy of note is that the Greek word for the "marks" ("stigmata") signified the branding applied to a slave; and in that sense it may also affirm Paul's apostolic status as "servant" or "slave" of Christ (1:10).

In 2 Corinthians 11:26 Paul writes ". . . danger from my own people, danger from Gentiles. . . ." He then writes later in the very same sentence of "toil and hardship." The same word that is translated "toil" there is translated as "trouble" here in Galatians 6:17 in the NRSV. It can mean work or labor or any sort of distress or difficulty. Comparing 2 Corinthians 11:26–27 with Galatians 6:17 is interesting in that the former references both "my own people" and "Gentiles" and enumerates several difficulties and stressful situations. Has Paul here simply had enough? Is he saying, "no more!"? Perhaps so, in a pointed and telling way.

Second Corinthians 4:7–10 is another helpful passage in understanding the second part of the verse and the passage on a whole. In verse 10 Paul brings the full statement to a close with the words: ". . . always carrying in the body the death of Jesus, so that the life of Jesus may also be made visible in our bodies." He does, apparently, carry such "marks." It proves that his God-revealed (Gal. 1:10–13), Christ-centered gospel (1:6–7) is the real deal, and he is its apostle. To counter him and his message is to step outside of the new creation (6:16) and outside of "the only thing that counts" in Christian life and Christian community (5:6).

Also of interest is the consistency of the qualifier "of Jesus" in both 2 Corinthians and here. Galatians 6:17 is the only place where the bare "of Jesus" is used and, perhaps, points to the actual sufferings of the earthly Jesus as model for faith/faithfulness (2:16–21; 5:6).

Verse 6:18 appears as a much more standard benediction at the close of a letter of Paul, especially in comparison to the unique blessing of 6:16. A couple of items jump out here. First, there is the address to "brothers and sisters" or, perhaps better, "siblings." That occurs only here among the benedictions within the letters of Paul and is apt given its recurrence throughout the letter and given one of the overarching metaphors and arguments within the letter, which is that "we" all "might receive adoption as children" (4:6) and assume the role of "heir" (4:7). Second, the placement of "spirit" is not unique here among Paul's letters (see Phil. 4:23 and Phlm. 25), but is also particularly apt. As indicated directly in 5:25 and indirectly in 6:16, life in/among Christian community is all about following the Spirit. Verse 6:1, as we have seen, marks the members of the community as "Spiritual ones" and directs them to act "in a spirit of gentleness." Here Paul makes the neat and profound connection between the individual('s) spirit and *the* Spirit. And so Paul brings this extraordinary letter to a close. It is about the Spirit, the action of Jesus Christ, the community ("siblings"), and spirits of individuals in relationship with each other in active faithfulness.

Works Cited

All quotations from the Bible, including the Apocryphal/Deuterocanonical Books, are from the NRSV unless otherwise noted.

All quotations from the Dead Sea Scrolls are available in G. Vermes, trans., *The Complete Dead Sea Scrolls in English*, rev. ed. London: Penguin, 2004.

All quotations from ancient Greek and Latin literature, including Josephus and Philo, are from the editions of the Loeb Classical Library (Cambridge: Harvard University Press) unless otherwise noted.

Barclay, John M.G. *Obeying the Truth: A Study of Paul's Ethics in Galatians*. Edinburgh: T and T Clark, 1988.

Bauer, Walter, Frederick W. Danker, W. F. Arndt, and F. W. Gingrich (BADG), *Greek-English Lexicon of the New Testament and Other Early Christian Literature*, 3rd ed. Chicago: The University of Chicago Press, 2000.

Betz, Hans Dieter. *Galatians: A Commentary on Paul's Letter to the Churches in Galatia*. Hermeneia. Philadelphia: Fortress Press, 1979.

Cousar, Charles. *Reading Galatians, Philippians, and 1 Thessalonians: A Literary and Theological Commentary*. Reading the New Testament series. Macon: Smyth and Helwys, 2001.

Dunn, James D. G. *Jesus, Paul, and the Law: Studies in Mark and Galatians*. London: SPCK, 2000.

Hogan, Pauline Nigh. *No Longer Male and Female: Interpreting Galatians 3:28 in Early Christianity*. Library of New Testament Studies. London: T. & T. Clark, 2008.

Martyn, J. Louis. *Galatians: A New Translation with Introduction and Commentary*. The Anchor Bible, 33A. New York: Doubleday, 1997.

Meeks, Wayne A. *The First Urban Christians: The Social World of the Apostle Paul.* New Haven and Yale: Yale University Press, 1983.

Neusner, Jacob. *Confronting Creation: How Judaism Reads Genesis, An Anthology of Genesis Rabbah.* Columbia: University of South Carolina Press, 1991.

———. *Genesis Rabbah: The Judaic Commentary on the Book of Genesis, A New American Translation,* v. 2. Brown Judaic Studies, 105. Atlanta: Scholars Press, 1985.

Segal, Alan. "Response: Some Aspects of Conversion and Identity Formation," pp. 184–90 in Richard Horsley, ed., *Paul and Politics: Ekklesia, Israel, Imperium, Interpretation: Essays in Honor of Krister Stendahl.* Harrisburg, PA: Trinity Press International, 2000.

Stendahl, Krister. "The Apostle Paul and the Introspective Conscience of the West," pp. 78–96 in *Paul among Jews and Gentiles.* Philadelphia: Fortress Press, 1976.

For Further Reading

Bassler, Jouette M. *Navigating Paul: An Introduction to Key Theological Concepts.* Louisville, KY: Westminster John Knox Press, 2007.

Park, Eung Chun. *Either Jew or Gentile: Paul's Unfolding Theology of Inclusivity.* Louisville, KY: Westminster John Knox Press, 2003.

Segal, Alan F. *Paul the Convert: The Apostolate and the Apostasy of Saul the Pharisee.* New Haven, CT: Yale University Press, 1990.

Watson, Francis. *Paul, Judaism, and the Gentiles: Beyond the New Perspective.* Grand Rapids: Wm. B. Eerdmans, 2007.

CPSIA information can be obtained at www.ICGtesting.com
Printed in the USA
LVOW05s1942071213

364249LV00004B/355/P